The Manager as Coach

Recent Titles in
The Manager as . . . Series

The Manager as Change Leader
Ann Gilley

The Manager as Mentor
Michael J. Marquardt and Peter Loan

The Manager as Politician
Jerry W. Gilley

The Manager as Facilitator
Judy Whichard and Natalie L. Kees

The Manager as Leader
B. Keith Simerson and Michael L. Venn

The Manager as Motivator
Michael Kroth

The Manager as Coach

Jerry W. Gilley and Ann Gilley

The Manager as. . .

Westport, Connecticut
London

Library of Congress Cataloging-in-Publication Data

Gilley, Jerry W.
  The manager as coach / Jerry W. Gilley and Ann Gilley.
      p. cm. — (The manager as—, ISSN 1555–7480)
  Includes bibliographical references and index.
  ISBN-10: 0–275–99290–X (alk. paper)
  ISBN-13: 978–0–275–99290–3 (alk. paper)
  1. Employees—Coaching of. 2. Employee motivation. 3. Supervision of
employees. I. Gilley, Ann Maycunich. II. Title.
  HF5549.5.C53G55 2007
658.3′124—dc22   2006032996

British Library Cataloguing in Publication Data is available.

Library of Congress Catalog Card Number: 2006032996
ISBN-10: 0–275–99290–X
ISBN-13: 978–0–275–99290–3
ISSN: 1555–7480

First published in 2007

Praeger Publishers, 88 Post Road West, Westport, CT 06881
An imprint of Greenwood Publishing Group, Inc.
www.praeger.com

Printed in the United States of America

The paper used in this book complies with the
Permanent Paper Standard issued by the National
Information Standards Organization (Z39.48–1984).

10 9 8 7 6 5 4 3 2 1

Contents

Publisher's Note

The backbone of every organization, large or small, is its managers. They guide and direct employees' actions, decisions, resources and energies. They serve as friends and leaders, as motivators and disciplinarians, as problem solvers and counselors, and as partners and directors. Managers serve as liaisons between executives and employees, interpreting the organization's mission and realizing its goals. They are responsible for performance improvement, quality, productivity, strategy, *and* execution— through the people who work for and with them. All too often, though, managers are thrust into these roles and responsibilities without adequate guidance and support. MBA programs provide book learning but little practical experience in the art of managing projects and people; at the other end of the spectrum, exceptional talent in one's functional area does not necessarily prepare the individual for the daily rigors of supervision. This series is designed to address those gaps directly.

The Manager as . . . series provides a unique library of insights and information designed to help managers develop a portfolio of outstanding skills. From mentor to marketer, politician to problem solver, coach to change leader, each book provides an introduction to the principles, concepts, and issues that define the role; discusses the evolution of recent and current trends; and guides the reader through the dynamic process of assessing their strengths and weaknesses and creating a personal development plan. Featuring diagnostic tools, exercises, checklists, case examples, practical tips, and recommended resources, the books in this series will help readers at any stage in their careers master the art and science of management.

ONE

Introduction to Performance Coaching

Everyone's a coach.

—Don Shula

Or at least everyone has the potential to be a coach. But why bother? Consider the conditions businesses face—fierce competition, rapidly changing environment, scarce resources, demanding customers, and contemporary problems unresolved by old solutions. These factors and more create new rules of engagement for which many managers and employees are ill-prepared. Why performance coaching? Because coaches are in the business of constant and rapid change, strategy, new challenges, innovative solutions, talent management, and quick decision making. If you face similar challenges in your work environment, coaching may be for you.

WHY COACH?

Skeptics claim that performance coaching is simply the newest management fad. To the contrary, leaders throughout history have used coaching techniques to develop and enhance performance of themselves and others. Realizing that they cannot excel without the guidance of a coach, many have credited coaches (whom they have also called mentors, sages, guides, or confidants) with contributing to their success. Presidents, monarchs, heads of state, world-class athletes, and performers have surrounded and continue to surround themselves with experts on whom they rely for advice, guidance, feedback, support, reinforcement, encouragement, challenge, confrontation, instruction, observation, and more.

And yet, the more things change, the more they stay the same. We face the same challenges today that we faced centuries ago: scarcity of resources (and corresponding battles), varying levels of individual talent, the need to improve performance, distribution complexities, competition, and so on. Coaches are needed to

- institute and manage change,
- model mastery,
- provide ongoing training,
- mold values, character, and commitment,
- model collaboration and team building,[1]
- improve individual and team performance,
- creatively solve problems,[2] and
- assess and strategically deploy human talent.

MANAGERIAL MALPRACTICE

Most of us have worked for managers who shouldn't be in their positions—they create work environments full of fear and paranoia, and they defy us to challenge their authority. We've been victimized by managers who are abusive and indifferent toward employees and who possess superior attitudes, have poor interpersonal skills, refuse to delegate, have little or no patience, and fail to conduct developmental evaluations or develop their people. These managers criticize employees' efforts or personalities rather than confront their work performance. In short, we've all experienced the manager from hell—that individual who exhibits some or all of the characteristics just described. As a result, organizations fail to achieve satisfactory results—employee morale and productivity remain low, turnover is high or rising, the quality of products and services is poor, and costs rise. Managerial malpractice is running rampant.

Simply stated, managerial malpractice occurs when firms hire, retain, and use managers who are unqualified, poorly trained, misguided, or inadequately prepared.[3] These managers lack the interpersonal skills required to interact effectively with employees, enhance commitment, or improve individual, team, or organizational performance. This problem has plagued organizations for years and has become the Achilles' heel of literally thousands of firms. Poor managerial hiring and promotion practices, lack of managerial development initiatives, inadequate human resource planning, inefficient organizational structures, and ineffective policies and procedures are seldom addressed by organizations—and if left unchecked, they prevent firms from achieving the results they desire. Economic downturns and fierce competition highlight the problem, which manifests itself in inadequate or falling productivity, revenues, market share, or share price.

Leaders and managers in some firms believe that employees are disposable and easily replaced. Their policies and procedures demonstrate a revolving-door philosophy toward human resources, who are mere consumables. When this philosophy predominates, managers' treatment of employees lacks dignity and respect because of the belief that people are throwaways and that an abundant quantity of qualified replacements exists. In some circumstances, employees *are* inadequately prepared to perform the activities necessary to produce acceptable business results; however, an overall callous organizational attitude further compounds an already bad situation, which can lead to costly turnover. Employee turnover disrupts the organization and its personnel, possibly damaging individuals because of the traumatic nature of these experiences.

The majority of employees have experienced managerial malpractice up close and personal. But how does people know when their organization is suffering from managerial malpractice?

We identified the symptoms of managerial malpractice earlier in this section. When an organization exhibits one or more symptoms, managerial malpractice is present. How many of these symptoms must persist before organizations recognize them as problems? When do firms take corrective action, and how? The question of when varies by firm, as does the subject of how. However, one fact remains indisputable. Organizations with talented, effective management teams weather cyclical business changes more favorably than those victimized by managerial malpractice. A common thread (and antidote) among many world-class, successful organizations is performance coaching.

WHAT IS PERFORMANCE COACHING?

Performance coaching is a partnership that equips individuals with the tools they need to succeed. Most important, coaching enables people to develop themselves.[4] An old and familiar Chinese proverb is "Give a man a fish and you feed him for a day. Teach a man to fish and you feed him for a lifetime." The same is true of the performance coaching process. To put it briefly, managers as coaches partner with employees in honest, collaborative exchanges regarding performance that focus on expanding excellence via individual learning, growth, and development. Coaching endows individuals with the ability to approach or react to opportunities, threats, and other events in a confident, reflective, powerful way. We explore the details further in chapters 2 and 3.

MYTHS OF PERFORMANCE COACHING

As with any concept, misconceptions regarding coaching's purposes, application, implementation, and benefits abound (see Table 1.1). Common myths about coaching include the following: coaching is too time-consuming; it is only necessary for new employees; and coaching and management are the same thing.

Coaching Is Too Time-Consuming

A common misconception about performance coaching is that it requires hours and hours of private tutoring with employees. Although personal feedback and attention are important elements of performance coaching, an effective performance coach's primary responsibility is to create conditions that enable individuals to develop on their own. A performance coach often spends time training employees; however, the majority of employees' personal development should be based on their individualized growth and development plans (see chapter 3).

Performance coaching consists of more than providing feedback, advice, or recommendations. It is a process that relies on a person's insight into his

Table 1.1
Coaching Is . . .

Coaching is . . .	Coaching is not . . .
Ongoing	A one-time event
Developmental	Planning, directing, organizing, controlling
Participative, collaborative	Dictatorial
Equipping, empowering, supportive, counseling	Enabling
Honest	Abusive
Teaching	Forcing
Mentoring	Manipulating
Evaluating	Criticizing

or her behavior and a systematic, effective approach to guiding that person to change. Because feedback is the foundation of performance coaching, it requires advanced interpersonal and communication skills as well as active listening, analysis techniques, and performance analysis interpretations.

Coaching Is Only Necessary for New Employees

Although new hires often do require additional attention, no one is exempt from the need for coaching. New employees need orientation, training, mentoring, goals, clear expectations, advice, guidance, feedback, growth and development plans, and career counseling. So, too, do experienced personnel, managers, and executives. Executive coaching, for example, is a growing field and line of business. Continuous improvement of the organization necessitates unremitting dedication to growth and renewal of its members at all levels. World-class athletes practice constantly under the tutelage of experts—in short, they are coached throughout their careers. Those who aspire to work for world-class organizations are no different. They seek the advice, guidance, and feedback of informal or formal coaches.

Performance Coaching and Management Are the Same Thing

Although effective managers exhibit many of the qualities and engage in many of the activities carried out by performance coaches, coaching encompasses a more holistic approach. Managers typically focus on current organizational objectives, jobs, and tasks, whereas coaches exemplify a future-oriented commitment to growth and development of self, personnel, and organization. This represents a fundamental difference in philosophy between management, which is organization-centered, and coaching, which concentrates on development of people. These differences will be explored further in chapter 2.

BENEFITS OF PERFORMANCE COACHING

The benefits of performance coaching are numerous for organizations, managers, and employees. Performance coaching is a developmental process in which all personnel grow and develop, improve their performance, and advance their careers (see Table 1.2).

Performance Coaching Benefits to Individuals

For employees, performance coaching encourages challenges, opportunities, and growth. Coaching provides employees with

- better relationships with their managers, including appreciation of the managers' expertise;
- improved self-esteem via challenging and rewarding assignments, positive feedback, and encouragement;
- an environment that encourages growth and development;
- opportunities to develop to their fullest potential;
- opportunities to influence the ways in which they relate to work, the work environment, and the organization;
- greater job, or career, satisfaction; and
- being treated as human beings with complex sets of needs and values, all of which are important in their work and lives.[5]

Performance Coaching Benefits for Managers

Managers aid their organizations and personnel through coaching activities. In return, they reap the following benefits:

- They gain better understanding of their employees' skills, strengths, and areas needing development for current and future assignments, which also enables succession planning.

Table 1.2
Benefits of Coaching

Benefits to . . .		
Individuals	Managers	Organizations
Better relationship with manager	Better relationship with employees	Fewer complaints, grievances, and lawsuits
Self-esteem	Understanding of employees' strengths and weaknesses	Better communication among all levels
Job satisfaction	Motivated, productive workforce	Capacity, productivity, resilience, and superior results
Advancement and career opportunities	Superior results through their people	Enhanced collaboration, teamwork, and competitiveness
Individualized attention	Enhanced interpersonal and managerial skills	Improved culture and work environment
Treatment as a unique being	Opportunities to serve personnel	Organizational learning
Personal and professional growth and development	Career opportunities	Competitive advantage through people

- They encounter opportunities to better serve their personnel through learning facilitation, persuasion, mentoring, and leading.
- They receive superior results from people (e.g., higher sales levels, better customer service, greater production, fewer errors, and so on).
- They have a more motivated and productive workforce.
- They engage in enhanced problem solving as a result of collaboration.
- They are energized, motivated, and challenged to become the best managers and leaders they can be.
- They take on increasingly difficult managerial assignments, which initiates change within the firm.
- They are perceived as human beings rather than as resources in the productivity process.
- They enhance their own interpersonal skills.

Performance Coaching Benefits for the Organization

Ultimately, organizations improve as personnel improve, just as a rising tide raises all ships. Organizational benefits of coaching include

- better communications between and among leaders, managers, and personnel;
- improved performance and effectiveness;
- improved capability, which is a firm's ability to establish internal structures and processes that influence its members to create organization-specific competencies and which thus enables the organization to adapt to changing customer and strategic needs";[6]
- increased competitiveness through achievement of strategic goals and objectives;
- enhanced creativity, problem solving, and decision making;
- more accurate HR and succession planning (the result of assessment of talent, growth; and development plans);
- healthy employees who are more qualified to lead the firm to long-term success, the result of the aggregate growth, development, reflection, and renewal abilities of personnel;
- transfer of individuals' enhanced knowledge, skills, and abilities to the firm (organizational learning);
- development and maintenance of the most important systems and linkages needed for improving performance, readiness, efficiency, and effectiveness;
- adaptation of developmental and leadership strategies that optimize the contributions of all employees;

- enhanced collaboration, teamwork, and the ability to capitalize on synergy to produce results; and
- competitive advantage through people, which is nearly impossible for rivals to duplicate.

CONCLUSION

The need for and benefits of performance coaching are clear. The times demand it, organizations and their personnel need it, and managers are capable. Next, we explore the fundamentals of coaching—what it is, who coaches are, and what they do.

TWO

Nature of
Performance Coaching

WHAT IS PERFORMANCE COACHING?

Performance coaching involves establishing a collegial partnership between managers and their staff for the purpose of improving performance. Through teaching, mentoring, counseling, and providing feedback, managers inspire and motivate their employees to succeed. In this way, performance coaching is the "process of equipping people with the tools, knowledge, and opportunities they need to develop themselves and become more effective."[1] Quite simply, performance coaches do not develop people—they equip people to develop themselves.

Key elements of coaching are awareness and responsibility.[2] The *Concise Oxford Dictionary* defines awareness as "conscious, not ignorant, having knowledge." *Webster's Dictionary* adds, "Awareness implies having knowledge of something through alertness in observing or in interpreting what one sees, hears, feels, etc." Awareness can be raised or heightened considerably through focused attention and practice, a common tenet of coaching. Responsibility is crucial to establishing success because commitment rises when a person truly chooses to take responsibility for his or her thoughts and actions.[3] Conversely, individual acceptance is low when someone is *ordered* to be responsible. Thus, both coach and subject must enter into the relationship with clear expectations of each other's behavior and roles.

Performance coaching is a continuous process of equipping individuals with the tools, knowledge, and opportunities they need to develop themselves and to be more effective. The performance coaching process involves five strategies:

1. Forging a partnership—building trust and understanding so that people want to work with you
2. Inspiring commitment—developing insight and motivation so that people focus their energy on goals that matter
3. Growing skills—building new competencies to ensure people know how to do what is required
4. Promoting persistence—developing a "never say die" attitude among managers and employees
5. Shaping the environment—creating conditions that foster growth and development[4]

The primary role for performance coaches is that of performance-improvement agent.[5] Insightful performance coaches understand that performance improvement is a constant in today's organizations. Moreover, performance coaches realize that helping individuals improve their renewal capacity and resilience improves organizational success. As a performance-improvement agent, a performance coach

- questions the status quo,
- feels challenged by the unknown,
- looks at things from new perspectives,
- takes risks,
- is willing to make mistakes and learn from them,
- is driven by personal integrity,
- inspires others to be their best,
- is future-oriented and cautiously optimistic,
- looks for new opportunities in the performance-improvement process,
- pursues useful alliances and networks that enhance cooperation and results,
- rehearses scenarios thoroughly before making decisions,
- guides persons and systems into new developmental growth,
- imagines new ways to look at things,
- presents ideas and makes them convincing,
- confronts behaviors that shut down human energy and hope,
- nurtures employees in transition, and
- facilitates learning, training, and referrals.[6]

PURPOSES OF PERFORMANCE COACHING

The performance coaching process improves individual performance, helps people work through change, assists individual and team problem solving, and helps individuals, teams, and the organization secure desired results.

Improving Performance

Improving performance is a five-stage process focused on performance outputs, the results required by the organization. Coaches are intimately involved throughout each stage, constantly assessing, communicating, and providing and receiving feedback. The five stages are as follows:

1. Determine outputs—Identify the required performance outputs and communicate them to employees. Clearly distinguish what is required of each individual as well as what is required of the aggregate team.
2. Identify activities—Identify the activities required to produce a given output, including the step-by-step tasks or engagements (processes) necessary to produce a product or service. Performance activities reflect the best practices employees will use on the job. Training may be required during this stage.
3. Set standards—Identify and communicate performance standards that must be met or exceeded regarding performance outputs or activities. These standards serve as criteria that can be used when determining whether a performance output has been produced at an acceptable level or whether a job has been completed correctly. These performance standards represent a blueprint for executing the job task or providing performance deliverables. Demonstration and modeling are appropriate during this stage.
4. Compare performance—Compare an individual's current performance with established standards. This step determines whether there exists a serious deviation in the execution of a given job or a difference between actual and desired performance outputs. During this stage, coaches provide developmental feedback.
5. Create and implement action plans—Develop action plans to improve the way employees perform a specific task or set of activities (even if actual performance already exceeds established standards). Working collaboratively with employees, performance coaches craft plans for helping individuals further enhance existing skills, acquire new ones, or extinguish ineffective behaviors.

Embracing Change

Change is the heart of performance improvement. Improvement cannot and will not occur without change. Understanding the fundamentals of change and human reactions to it enables coaches to leverage their knowledge of the individual and the organization to make change happen.

Individuals are inherently resistant to change, a fact not lost on performance coaches. Overcoming resistance and improving performance requires that coaches

- enhance their change-management skills;
- communicate, communicate, communicate;
- educate others regarding the specifics of the change;
- involve those impacted in designing and implementing the change;
- understand causes of resistance and take corrective action;
- provide stress-management programs and techniques; and
- celebrate success and reward participants who change.[7]

The process of change itself proves to be as unpredictable, taxing, and stimulating as those people involved. Although many change models exist, none can guarantee success. Coaches persevere through strategic planning and fierce dedication to the mission, fully realizing the complexities of change and individuals' reactions. A commonly engaged model of change includes the following steps:

1. Lead the change.
2. Create a shared need.
3. Shape a vision.
4. Mobilize commitment.
5. Change systems and structures (to support the new way).
6. Monitor progress.
7. Make change last; integrate it into the culture.[8]

Solving Problems

Life is fraught with problems, sometimes defying us to oppose. Fortunately, performance coaching proves an effective means by which to creatively solve problems. Performance coaches employ a variety of problem-solving techniques that challenge others to think "outside the box." One of the most effective approaches to resolving problems includes the following steps: (1) identifying the problem, (2) isolating the root cause of the problem, (3) generating possible solutions, (4) analyzing solutions,

(5) selecting a viable solution, (6) implementing the solution, and (7) evaluating the solution.

Although a common and proven approach, it is important to remember that employees are responsible for integrating the problem-solving process on the job. They must be encouraged to systematically execute each step of the process. Problem solving thus becomes the responsibility of every individual rather than a technique employed for them.

Securing Desired Results

Perhaps the most important benefit of the performance coaching process is that it helps the firm achieve the results it needs. Desired results may include increased sales revenue, greater productivity, better customer service, improved quality and efficiency, or fewer production defects, to name a few. Managers cannot obtain desired results by themselves—they rely on their staff. This is where classic management techniques begin to fall apart because directing, organizing, and controlling may not produce positive results. Fortunately, making the transformation from manager to performance coach offers the process necessary for securing desired results through people.

COACHES: WHO ARE THEY? WHAT DO THEY DO?

Who is a coach? They're found everywhere—at all levels of the organization and occupying all positions. Coaches have been described as generalists who function in a variety of roles to guide their clients, as change agents who facilitate all phases of the change process, and as communicators who are articulate and convincing and who build consensus.[9] We believe that coaches are also specialists who possess expertise in a certain area (e.g., marketing, customer service, or change) and strategists constantly looking forward as they plan deployment of resources (see Table 2.1).

Characteristics and Actions of Performance Coaches

Most of us have been coached at some point in our lives. In our research during the past several years (including discussions with individuals and focus groups), people have cited athletics as the most frequent coaching venue, although some have listed events such as music practice or job interviewing as instances during which they've been coached. When asked to describe their past coaches, participants often combine a coach's characteristics

Table: 2.1
Coaches: Who They Are, What They Do

Who They Are	*What They Do*
Generalists	Understand human behavior Draw from their own vast, varied experiences
Specialists	Possess expertise in a certain area
Communicators	Speak clearly and consistently Give messages that are compelling and convincing Exhibit integrity Are sometimes charismatic
Change agents	Seek constant improvement Take risks Pursue top talent Understand how to help others work through change Are willing to try new approaches Create alliances to achieve success Facilitate learning
Strategists	Focus on long-term success Link short-term plans to long-term strategies Assess strengths and deploy resources accordingly (to maximize contribution)

with his or her actions. The following list, by no means all-inclusive, contains the most common responses. Essentially, a coach does the following:

- Motivates
- Teaches
- Models behavior and performance
- Chooses the best person for the team based on his or her abilities
- Pushes and brings out the best in employees
- Is decisive
- Provides recognition and rewards—of accomplishments, development, progression, and improvement
- Sees potential in all and recognizes that everyone has strengths
- Treats everyone as an individual and gives chances and options
- Serves as a role model
- Cares—about what he or she is doing and about the individuals and the team
- Provides feedback—people like to know what they're doing wrong or well
- Knows what he or she is working toward—the goal or vision
- Sets goals, seeing the big picture
- Coaches sometimes for really small things and sometimes for a championship

- Has high standards and expectations, which are not necessarily harsh but consistent
- Shows respect
- Challenges you and helps you stretch yourself
- Listens
- Has compassion—is soft on the inside, even if tough on the outside
- Communicates verbally, nonverbally, frequently, and well
- Is equitable and fair
- Has technical expertise appropriate to what he or she is coaching
- Helps you become independent, in that you learn what the coach has to teach, and you move on
- Reflects
- Helps take you from one point in your abilities to the next
- Is supportive of individuals, even if they make different choices
- Allows failure and uses it as a learning tool
- Is your biggest cheerleader
- Puts you, or the team, first

The preceding list reveals the true nature of coaching—that of devotion to the success of others. Some research indicates that effective performance coaches embrace humanistic values, believing that organizations should serve humans, not the reverse.[10] This view maintains that performance coaches are supportive of initiatives that help employees

- be more involved in decisions that directly affect them;
- be assertive regarding their needs, if not their rights;
- plan their careers;
- become more a part of the work group;
- obtain more interesting jobs or enrich the ones they have;
- have opportunities for additional training, education, and personal development;
- be more involved with their superiors in establishing the objectives and quotas they are expected to reach, and;
- in general, receive respect and fair treatment.

Performance coaches create environments that bring the best out of others, find opportunities to build bridges to the future, connect what is to what might be, and work toward what is possible using imagination, vision, and motivation as resources. Performance coaches link inner purpose to organizational objectives, inspire others to be more effective, and question the status quo. They seek creative solutions to complex problems and facilitate professional and organizational development. Coaches are responsible for creating fear-free environments, expecting success of others, encouraging excellence, asking questions, and allowing individuals to make mistakes and govern their own performance.[11] Finally, performance coaches guide individuals through necessary transitions, encourage cooperation, develop alliances and linkages with common goals, and serve as a catalyst for renewal and resilience.

Management versus Coaching

One question we ask during focus groups is, "What's the difference between a manager and a coach?" Without exception, respondents state that an effective manager exhibits the same qualities and engages in the same activities as an effective coach—with one critical difference. Coaches are perceived as putting the needs of the employee or team above their own; managers are seen as self-serving. This perception, real or not, creates a level of trust for coaches and a powerful psychological contract. The mistrust of managers and their intentions builds a barrier that managers are rarely able to breach.

Core Values of Performance Coaches

Performance coaching is based on six core values.[12] The first is *personal identity*, which involves defining yourself by developing a positive self-esteem, confidence, inner motivation, clear ego boundaries, self-respect, and courage. The second core value, *achievement*, involves improving yourself. This is enhanced by reaching goals, enhancing your skills, completing projects, working, winning, playing in organized sports, having ambition, getting results and recognition, and being purposeful. The third core value, *intimacy*, involves knowing and sharing yourself. Intimacy is demonstrated through loving, bonding, caring, touching, engaging in friendships, parenting, and showing empathy for others. The fourth core value is *play and creativity*, which involves expressing oneself. This can be demonstrated by being imaginative, intuitive, playful, spontaneous, original, expressive, humorous, artistic, celebrative, funny, curious, and childlike. The fifth core value, *searching for meaning*, entails discovering oneself. Searching for meaning includes finding wholeness, unity, integrity, peace, spirituality, trust in the flow of life, inner wisdom, a sense of transcendence, and purpose. The sixth core value, *compassion and contribution*, involves giving of oneself. This is demonstrated through volunteering, helping, leaving the world a better place, bequeathing, being generous, serving, caring socially and environmentally, institution building, and engaging in activism. These core values represent our passions. People often shift throughout the adult years from familiar, accomplished value areas to new, challenging ones.[13]

BARRIERS TO PERFORMANCE COACHING

The benefits of coaching to individuals, teams, and organizations are well-known. So why isn't coaching more widespread? Obstacles abound. Barriers to coaching exist at all levels; some of the most common are

- inherent resistance to change,
- lack of support from management,
- lack of trust,
- poor attitude or arrogance,
- dysfunctional culture,
- inadequate systems to support coaching,
- lack of training for coaches,
- differing values,
- lack of consequences for failure to coach or for poor performance,
- lack of rewards for coaching success, and
- lack of commitment to change.

OVERCOMING BARRIERS TO PERFORMANCE COACHING

Obstacles to coaching are as diverse as individuals and as complex as the largest organization. Suffice it to say that no "one size fits all" strategy will work. Overcoming barriers or resistance to coaching mandates understanding of the opposing forces at work, both individually and organizationally. Barriers such as prior personal experiences or organizational culture in particular demand patience and consideration on the part of coaches. Following are some strategies for overcoming barriers to coaching:

Take it slow—Have patience. Culture change often takes years, and simply saying something won't make it so. Model the behavior, walk the talk, and allow others to see or experience the benefits of coaching.
Remove obstacles in the system—Certain organizational policies, procedures, processes, or reporting relationships by their very nature hinder coaching efforts. Identify and eliminate these.
Engage leadership—Mobilize leaders and engender their support of coaching efforts at all levels. Encourage them to verbalize their support and model performance coaching.

Provide training—Assess the current coaching skill level of leaders, managers, and employees, and provide opportunities for enhancement of their coaching skills.

Reward coaching efforts—Recognize and reward coaches and their subjects for their efforts.

THE PERFORMANCE COACHING PROCESS

Some managers mistakenly believe that performance coaching is simply a formalized feedback approach. On the contrary, it is a complex, intricate process that includes several important roles and activities that must be adopted in order to help employees solve problems, improve performance, embrace change, and achieve desired results. Performance coaching reduces managerial malpractice while allowing organizations to better manage performance.

At its core, performance coaching is a person-centered management technique that requires face-to-face communications, personal involvement with employees, and establishment of rapport. This is an active process requiring constant shifts from one role to another, transforming managers from passive observers to active participants with their staff. Performance coaching is based on good questioning, listening, feedback, and facilitation skills as opposed to autocratic, controlling techniques.

Observation of performance remains the primary information-gathering tool of performance coaches.[14] When employees perform well, positive reinforcement is appropriate. Failing to perform adequately prompts the performance coach to investigate cause and furnish the individual with instructions that enable successful execution in the future. Performance coaches then follow up, thus making certain that corrective action has been taken.

Coaching Continuums

Coaching opportunities generally call for behaviors that fall along two continuums (see chapter 3, Figure 3.1). These two continuums can be combined to create a working model that illustrates the possible performance coaching roles encountered with staff. The horizontal continuum reveals asserting/encouraging behavior with employees, whereas the vertical continuum expresses partnering/directing behavior.

This model illustrates four primary roles, each of which represents a philosophical orientation toward performance coaching. For example, providing instruction or feedback requires the directive approach with employees— which can be represented by the coaching roles of trainer and performance appraiser. Other situations require a partnering approach, represented by the career advisor and strategist roles. Further definition of roles depends on the coach's perception of whether he or she should serve as a director or partner with personnel. Each role has a number of different outcomes associated with it, which is explained in further detail in chapter 3.

CONCLUSION

Certain organizations are fortunate enough to have individuals who see themselves not just as "bosses," but as performance coaches, taking the responsibility for

- providing personnel with training that applies directly to the job,
- helping individuals enhance their careers and solve problems,
- confronting employees in positive ways to improve their performance, and
- mentoring others to help them become the best they can be.

The result is motivated, productive employees ready to accept challenges and take initiative. This process is based on the synergistic relationship between performance coaches and their staff, which enhances self-esteem and productivity.

THREE

Roles and Responsibilities of Performance Coaches

The performance coaching process is based on the synergistic relationship between managers (performance coaches) and their employees, and it is designed to improve performance, enhance self-esteem, and increase productivity. The result is motivated, productive employees ready to accept challenges and take initiative.

Performance coaches are challenged to interact with a diverse body of employees and respond to a myriad of constantly changing situations. This dynamic environment forces managers to continually adapt their performance coaching styles. Employees' personalities, emerging conflicts, challenges, and fears combine with organizational pressures, goals, and competition to produce a state of constant change. Performance coaches know when to push, pull, or stand back.

CONTINUUMS OF PERFORMANCE COACHING

Coaching opportunities generally call for behaviors that fall along two continuums (see Figure 3.1). These two continuums can be combined to create a working relationship that illustrates the possible performance coaching roles encountered with employees. The horizontal continuum reveals

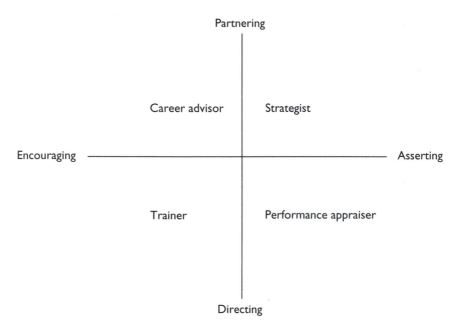

Figure 3.1 Performance Coaching Roles

asserting/encouraging behavior with employees, and the vertical continuum expresses partnering/advocating behavior.

This model illustrates four primary roles, each of which represents a philosophical orientation toward performance coaching. For example, the acts of providing feedback and conducting performance appraisals require performance coaches to be assertive, directive, and partnership-oriented with employees—which can be represented by the strategist and performance appraiser roles of performance coaching. Other situations require a supportive, encouraging, and directive approach, represented by the trainer and career advisor roles. Further definition of roles depends on the coach's perception of whether he or she should serve as an advocate or partner with employees. Each role has a number of different outcomes associated with it. Each is briefly explained in the following sections, with common outcomes identified (see Table 3.1).

Trainer

Performance coaching is characterized by several critical roles, one of the most important being that of a trainer. As trainers, performance coaches are directive, yet they operate as partners in performance improvement, using feedback and summary techniques to make certain that employees

Table 3.1
Performance Coach's Roles and Responsibilities

Roles	Responsibilities
Trainer	Facilitate learning
	Enhance resilience
Career advisor	Perform career analysis
	Assist with career planning
	Improve career opportunities
Strategist	Envision the future
	Sponsor change
	Problem-solve
	Engage in succession planning
Performance appraiser	Establish goals and standards
	Evaluate performance
	Provide feedback
	Conduct cause analysis
	Create growth and development plans
	Link compensation to growth and development
	Improve performance

fully grasp the concepts being taught (see Figure 3.1). When employees do not possess the knowledge, skills, or attitudes to appropriately perform their jobs, or when they are unable to properly sequence performance activities and tasks, it is appropriate for performance coaches to serve in the role of trainer. In this role, the coach is a one-on-one tutor with employees, responsible for sharing information that will ultimately impact employee growth and development. This traditionally comes in the form of on-the-job training, but can also include formal training activities.

In the trainer role, performance coaches present information that is meaningful as well as practical to their employees—and in a way that permits mastery. Employees must understand completely and be able to utilize their training in order for it to be significant. This may require the trainer to present one idea or concept at a time, often sequentially, rather than explaining the whole performance process in its entirety. To be an effective trainer, a performance coach must use feedback with frequent summaries to make certain that the learner has understood the information shared.

As trainers, performance coaches guide and direct employees, helping them in the acquisition of knowledge, skills, and appropriate attitudes. To be successful as trainers, performance coaches must appropriately utilize the communication process. Effective communication involves active listening, articulating clearly, speaking in terms that others understand, and soliciting feedback to ensure understanding.

In its simplest sense, learning facilitation can be thought of as the communication of experience. Experience may involve demonstrating how a specific skill improves the completion of a task or how new knowledge enables employees to better problem solve or analyze a performance situation. Sharing experience is most appropriate when employees don't have the knowledge or skills to do their jobs, don't know how to do their jobs, or don't understand their job responsibilities.

When these aforementioned circumstances are present, performance coaches should focus on learning activities that break down complicated tasks into small, manageable steps that enable less-experienced employees to master the steps and activities. Employees then learn how to perform tasks one step at a time. If training is successful, individuals will be able to perform the tasks adequately.

Learning is a very complex, complicated process requiring great skill and expertise. To master the role of trainer, performance coaches must incorporate three distinct elements into every training activity:

1. Arrange the training environment to maximize opportunities for communicating privately and without interruption.
2. Communicate in language easily understood by learners.
3. Present information one step at a time, allowing employees to apply the tasks or skills under realistic conditions, and allow time for review, reflection, and evaluation.

Career Advisor

Occasionally, performance coaches find it necessary to be supportive and serve as leaders with employees—engaging in the role of career advisor (see Figure 3.1). Career advising encourages performance coaches to share their experiences with employees, which helps individuals gain additional insight, understanding, and awareness that will be invaluable in the progression of their careers. Career advising allows employees to benefit from coaches' experiences, both the successes and failures—thus alleviating employees' fears, concerns, frustrations, and pains, while promoting celebration of successes and job accomplishments. The encouraging, supportive, and interactive nature of career advising is developmental because it helps performance coaches become more caring, sympathetic, and patient. In short, developing employees via career advising helps performance coaches grow as well.

Career advising is a process of ultimate sharing, providing you the opportunity to unlock the mysteries of the organization for your employees.[1]

Career advising helps employees avoid the costly mistakes and pitfalls so damaging to their careers. It can also help employees adjust to the organization's culture and better assimilate into the work environment.

Traditional managers who maintain an authoritative, noninvolved style based on the "my way or the highway" mentality have difficulty performing as career advisors. As career advisors, performance coaches value their relationships with their employees and strive to overcome managerial malpractice. Career advising, more than any other role, requires that managers develop a synergistic, self-esteeming relationship with their staff. They must also believe that the success of the organization is based on the success of its employees. When these attitudes are present, coaches function effectively as career advisors—and are on the road to overcoming the performance improvement challenge.

To be effective career advisors, managers must have substantial knowledge of the organization, including thorough understanding of its vision, direction, and long-range goals and objectives. They must also maintain an appropriate network that will enable employees to make critical contacts throughout the organization. Successful career advisors possess and share technical competence to help employees overcome skill deficiencies. Most successful career advisors possess a degree of charisma; employees are drawn to individuals who possess the ability to persuade others, and they like to be around people whose opinions and ideas are sought by other members of the organization. Career advisors must have credibility within the organization. Finally, to be effective career advisors, managers must be willing to bear responsibility for someone else's growth and development. At the heart of a career-advising relationship is an eagerness to improve others and help them become the best that they can be.

Career advisors support several activities for employee growth and development. Career advisors often serve as confidants in times of personal and professional difficulty, providing feedback, observation of performance, and personal reactions. Career advisors provide insight about the mission, goals, and strategic direction of an organization. They help employees develop political savvy and awareness that enable the employees to function effectively within the organization. Career advisors provide employees with insights into organizational philosophy, operations, and the functional system. They help employees with long-term career planning, growth, risk taking, and advancement opportunities. Career advisors enable their employees to participate in visible projects and programs that may further advance their careers. Finally, career advisors serve as honest, open, direct guides.

The relationship between employee and the organization is the core to employees' career development. This vital relationship often leads organizations to take one of two approaches when establishing career-development programs. They employ career-development specialists or assign career-development responsibilities directly to managers. The latter alternative appeals to many organizations because of its simplicity and cost benefits. It can also be argued that a manager's impact on an individual's career is greater than any other organizational factor. Thus, performance coaches are uniquely qualified to be career advisors:

- They benefit from having practical experience.
- They make realistic appraisals of organization opportunities.
- They use information from past performance evaluations to make realistic suggestions concerning career planning.
- They evaluate external economic opportunities.
- They have experienced similar career decisions and can be empathetic toward the employee.

Many hesitate to offer career advising to subordinates because they lack formal training in psychology or counseling and feel inadequate in the role. In addition, most managers have been promoted to positions with supervisory responsibility because of technical abilities and skills (e.g., financial or operational), not necessarily because of interpersonal competencies. Thus, when confronted with difficult or complex problems, performance coaches sometimes lack the competencies and abilities to correctly address them. The transition from technician to career advisor is difficult and often frustrating.

Research and experience show that most managers already possess many of the necessary interpersonal and human relations skills necessary in the career-advising process. Present skills can be further developed through study, training, and practice. For example, because most of a performance coach's time with employees is spent in verbal interactions, career advising can be an important developmental activity to enhance a leader's communication and interpersonal skills. Following are additional actions that can be taken to enhance one's skills as a career advisor:

- Develop knowledge of occupational information and career resource material.
- Develop an understanding of the different career theories and their applications.
- Take classes related to counseling theories, human relations, and counseling techniques.
- Subscribe to professional journals that publish articles on career development.
- Understand the elements of an effective relationship and how to build them.

- Develop good listening and questioning skills.
- Learn to respect the privacy and confidentiality of employees.

Developing these skills greatly enhances an individual's effectiveness and personal career development. For example, interpersonal skills aid during performance-appraisal interviews and other formal evaluations. Indirectly, then, pursuing the career-advising role provides you the opportunity to develop or enhance essential relationship skills. Quite simply, these skills can be used throughout your career and can increase your potential. In the final analysis, furthering interpersonal skills through the career-advising role benefits the organization while simultaneously advancing your competence.

Career advising serves at least eight valuable purposes, by

- providing assistance to individuals for career planning within the organization;
- conducting formal and informal individual assessments and interpretation;
- identifying relevant written resources and making information available to employees;
- identifying and coordinating organizational resources such as contacts, networks, or executive briefings;
- making referrals to external resources, such as counseling, testing, training, or outplacement services, as appropriate;
- providing support to performance coaches for career discussions or coaching with their employees;
- gathering demographic data regarding the needs of the organization, departments, or individuals; and
- consulting with organizational leaders on decisions affected by or affecting employee retention and development.

Strategist

One of the most important performance coaching roles is that of strategist. This critical leadership role enables you to facilitate change. As a strategist, you provide services that are valued by organizational leaders, which enables you to become a strategic business partner and improves your credibility within the organization by enhancing internal relationships. As such, you will have an enhanced awareness of the organization, create a mechanism for improving organizational effectiveness, and formulate a long-term decision-making strategy that fosters change.

As a strategist, you demonstrate your development skills, knowledge of organizational change, and ability to see the big picture. Strategists see the entire forest while maneuvering through the trees. They must lead the organization through uncharted territory in the quest for change.

Strategists are competent in assessing organizational needs using qualitative and quantitative methodologies, in developing and implementing organizational initiatives (e. g., performance management systems), and in evaluating the effectiveness of learning interventions and other initiatives. Strategists synthesize the input of others and translate it into action plans, set priorities that are consistent with organizational and departmental goals, direct the organization toward accomplishing its business goals, understand organizational systems, and identify relationships among departments. Accordingly, strategists are problem solvers who take an active role in the decision-making and change-management process. Their primary responsibility is making certain that the perceived problem is indeed the one that is critical to the organization. In other words, strategists spend the majority of their time determining the accuracy of a problem rather than providing solutions to problems that do not exist. A useful approach entails working with the problem as "defined" in such a way that more useful definitions emerge.

Strategists serve in the role of scout, responsible for developing an individual's readiness and commitment for organizational change. The following questions can be used as a guide in this process:

- How willing are my employees to implement change?
- What types of information do employees readily accept or resist?
- What are employees' attitudes toward change?
- To what extent will employees regard their contribution to overall organizational effectiveness as a legitimate and desirable objective?

Strategists have a thorough understanding of business fundamentals, including core business processes, basic business functions, and operating procedures. They also recognize the critical strategic factors affecting organizational competitiveness. Thus, they serve as strategic partners who have the ability to communicate the benefits provided to the organization by change strategies and interventions.

Organizations are complex systems made up of many divisions, departments, units, functions, job classifications, levels, and roles, each of which is essential to organizational success. One of a strategist's major roles is to help unify an organization by linking competitive divisions, departments, units, and people through a common set of guiding principles. These principles help determine the direction, purpose, and focus of an organization.

As system linkers, strategists are not directly involved in decision making, but instead help link parts of the organization together. System linkers establish connections between departments and people by communicating the value and importance of teamwork, thereby allowing employees to pull in the same direction to accomplish a common set of outcomes.

Organizational Effectiveness Enhancer. The ultimate purpose of the performance coaching process is to improve organizational effectiveness. Organizational effectiveness is sometimes defined as a firm's ability to adapt strategies and behaviors to further environmental change by maximizing contributions of the organization's human resources. Organizational effectiveness assumes that strategists are dedicated to developing and maintaining the most important systems and linkages to improve the firm's performance capacity.

When improving organizational effectiveness, strategists assist decision makers by using their client relationship–building skills, organizational development skills, and business understanding to identify the best solutions to the organization's problems. Simultaneously, they help organizational leaders overcome the barriers and obstacles that prevent change. Finally, they demonstrate their ability to assess organizational dynamics by managing the political environment.

Performance Appraiser

Performance coaches often find it necessary to be assertive partners with employees—engaging in the role of performance appraiser (see Figure 3.1). As a performance appraiser, you serve as an advocate during the performance-management process, act as a guide, provide and interpret information, give feedback, identify problems, facilitate solutions, and evaluate outcomes. Advocates are proactive "agents" who pioneer ways the organization can successfully implement the process. As scouts, performance coaches focus on the success of performance management, acting as performance-improvement ambassadors within the organization. Advocates for performance management demonstrate vision, possess credibility with other decision makers and stakeholders, and ask the organization to take risks that may seriously impact its future.

The primary purpose of performance appraisals is to provide a vehicle to discuss ways of enhancing employees' performance results. These conversations include an examination of employees' strengths, weaknesses, and areas for improvement. They become the focus of employee action plans and should be perceived as a long-term developmental strategy rather than a quick fix. Performance appraisals provide an excellent way of determining whether employees are producing adequate performance outputs and executing performance activities that meet or exceed performance standards.

As a performance appraiser, you ascertain satisfaction of internal and external constituents with performance outputs produced by employees. These reviews also present opportunities to discuss current and future developmental goals and objectives as well as how employees plan to improve their performance. Most important, performance appraisals are a vehicle for discussion of future growth and development activities that will enhance employees' abilities and competencies as well as advance their careers.

Benefits of Effective Performance Appraisals. Many employees fail to perform adequately because of barriers that prohibit exemplary performance. Therefore, performance appraisals do the following:

- Provide assessment of individuals' strengths, weaknesses, and areas for improvement
- Frame plans for growth and development
- Encourage feedback for improvement
- Help isolate performance obstacles and formulate strategies for overcoming them

As a result of these conversations, employees participate in discussions that improve the work environment and general conditions under which they are asked to perform.

At the core of every performance appraisal is the concept of feedback. Through feedback, those in the role of performance appraiser and those in the roles of career advisor and trainer engage in very similar activities. The fundamental difference is that the career advisor and trainer roles involve ongoing, minute-by-minute, day-by-day feedback opportunities, whereas performance appraisals are designed to be formal, summative evaluations. In some respects, the career advisor and trainer roles and the performance appraiser role are designed to achieve the same outcomes, which is the creation of action plans that improve employee performance. Accordingly, performance appraisals must be specific and timely in order for employees to make the types of corrections and improvements required to bring about desired business results.

Performance appraisals give you the opportunity to share your perspectives of your employees' performance and discuss means of improvement. In this way, performance appraisals serve a vital function within the organization.

In summary, performance appraisals provide individuals with feedback on their performance. They are useful in helping employees to recognize their strengths and achievements over a specific period of time and to identify areas where they can continue to grow and develop. Employees are able to define performance goals for the next six months to a year and review the "fit" between the organization's expectations and those of the employee. Performance appraisals help organizations make decisions regarding the performance of personnel and aid in construction of developmental and career-planning activities that enhance their work.

Transforming Performance Appraisals into Developmental Evaluations. One of the most important activities in which organizations can engage to overcome their performance shortfalls is to conduct regular (e.g., monthly, quarterly, semiannual, or annual) performance appraisals with each employee. Performance appraisals, often called performance reviews, give performance coaches the opportunity to judge the adequacy and quality of employees' work and create action plans that improve their performance. Unfortunately, the term "performance appraisal" restricts your ability to work collaboratively with employees in their development. To overcome this problem, we encourage performance coaches to treat performance appraisals as developmental evaluations.

Most organizations require regular evaluations in which supervisors assess employee performance. In theory, performance appraisals are supposed to be an effective assessment activity that rewards past performance, improves future work, and encourages career development. In reality, nothing could be further from the truth. Few organizations understand the importance and potential benefits of effective employee assessment—fewer still actually engage in effective evaluation.

Much of the disparity between performance-appraisal theory and practice lies in its execution. Many organizations rely on review forms that allow supervisors to painlessly evaluate their staff by assigning numbers to varied performance categories. This simple process can be more damaging than beneficial in that it prevents managers and their employees from thinking *developmentally*—that is, in a proactive way that focuses on individual personal and professional growth as opposed to past performance. Eliminating useless, wasteful performance-appraisal and review forms and substituting them with developmental evaluations provides managers the freedom to work collaboratively with their employees to maximize performance.

Developmental evaluations are in-depth explorations of (1) strengths and weaknesses, including knowledge, skill, abilities, and attitudes; (2) current and future goals and objectives, including career plans; (3) the "fit" between individual and organizational expectations; (4) whether stakeholder needs have been satisfied; and (5) how employee performance helps the organization achieve its strategic goals and objectives. This analysis reveals performance problems, solutions, and opportunities for employee growth and development.

PERFORMANCE COACHING RESPONSIBILITIES

Performance coaches have several responsibilities during the performance-management process. Many of the responsibilities are common to the specific role being executed, although all four roles are required to develop positive relations with employees. This means establishing positive working relations that foster interaction, support, and problem solving. Let's examine the specific responsibilities of each of the four roles of performance coaches.

As a performance coach, you ask reflective questions and help employees clarify or alter a given situation. Thus, you serve as a verifier and philosopher by asking reflective questions that improve the quality of change initiatives. Additionally, you observe the effectiveness of performance appraisals and reviews, the effects that performance standards have on quality and performance, and the impacts of job design and redesign activities.

Objective observation is a nondirective activity that enables you to witness the effects that change has on your employees and helps you guide them in their effort to overcome their resistance to change.

Responsibilities of Trainers

Facilitating Learning. A fundamental element of performance improvement is learning. It could be said that performance improvement does not take place until learning occurs. As a result, one of your most important responsibilities includes providing employees with learning opportunities, making certain they have access to references and tools needed during learning, and providing coaching and feedback when needed. Further, you are held accountable for conducting developmental evaluations, which enable employees to develop growth and development plans. Finally, you are responsible for linking compensation and rewards to learning (e. g., growth and development).

During the learning process, you are responsible for helping employees acquire new skills, knowledge, insights, awareness, and attitudes needed to implement change. For example, many employees will need skills or knowledge in problem solving, performance feedback, performance measurement, self-directed learning, interpersonal communication, causal analysis, listening, goal setting, conflicts resolution, and group diagnosis to be able to become independent employees. As they develop such skills or knowledge and apply what they have learned, employees will rely less on you.

On occasion, you facilitate learning activities to improve performance and increase productivity. In some situations, you are simply asked to recommend which learning processes are best. At other times, you may be asked to provide professional development activities to help your employees obtain needed knowledge and skills. Trainers rely on their understanding of the teaching–learning process and on appropriate use of instructional methods, application of experiential-learning activities, and their presentation, listening, and facilitating skills. Finally, you must have the ability to teach or create learning opportunities. This ability should not be reserved for formal classroom activities, but should be utilized on the job, during meetings, and within the mainstream of the overall change effort.

As a trainer, you have a special responsibility in assisting employees to use interactive, self-direct strategies for enhancing their own capability. In this case, the facilitator's role consists of helping employees shape their curiosities, challenging and developing their ideas for exploring and investigating, directing participants to useful resources, and linking people and ideas together to forge collaborative efforts.

Facilitating learning involves a transactional process, a relationship with a person that promotes initiative, autonomy, freedom, and growth. Six important principles of effective practice facilitate learning. Facilitation

1. relies upon voluntary participation, which means employees are highly self-motivated to learn and want to participate;
2. requires mutual respect among employees for each other's self-worth and uniqueness;
3. involves a collaborative spirit, a cooperative enterprise;
4. is a cyclical process (that is, employees reflect on a learning activity, and they engage in collaboratively analyzing the activity, in participating in a new activity, in further reflection and collaborative analysis of the activity, and so on);
5. fosters critical reflection, which involves having an attitude of healthy skepticism, developing critical thinking skills, and seeking to appreciate diversity and alternative points of view; and
6. nurtures self-directed, encouraged employees to become autonomous, proactive, initiating, and creative learners.[2]

Enhancing Resilience.   As a trainer, you are responsible for discovering ways to help employees strengthen the skills needed to adapt to change and thus remain resilient during ever-changing events. Trainers create an environment that provides support for discovery, change, and resiliency.

Consequently, your primary responsibility is to help the organization and its employees increase resilience by enhancing employees' capacity and ability to adapt to change.

Resilient employees realize when performance improvement is necessary or advantageous, use resources to creatively reframe a changing situation, improvise new approaches, or maneuver to gain an advantage. They take risks despite potentially negative consequences and draw important lessons from change-related experiences that are then applied to similar situations. They respond to disruption by investing energy in problem solving and teamwork, and they influence others to resolve conflicts.

Trainers strengthen their employees' adaptability to change for the purpose of improving their performance, both personally and professionally. Two approaches enhance resilience. First, employees increase their energy by developing adaptive skills. Second, they decrease energy and wasteful expenditures by accepting the inevitability of change and adjusting accordingly.

Responsibilities of Career Advisors

Career advisors have several important responsibilities, including (1) career analysis, (2) career planning, and (3) improving career opportunities.

Career Analysis. Individuals are ultimately responsible for the development of their own careers. Employees control decisions such as whether to remain in the organization, accept specific teaching or staff assignments, perform at acceptable levels, or engage in personal growth through learning activities or academic enhancement.

Career analysis begins with assessment of an individual's interests, passions, and strengths, which can then be channeled into an appropriate, exciting career path. As a career advisor, you are responsible for providing the means and the information to assist in individual career decision making and in creating a climate and culture that are conducive to career growth and development. Employees should take advantage of that climate and be aware of the important components of career development. They need to construct plans that enable them to accomplish their career goals, analyze potential career areas, determine whether they possess the skills, competencies, and knowledge necessary to be considered serious candidates for other positions, and get the feedback they need regarding the organization's philosophy of career development.

Career Planning.   Career planning's primary aim is to help employees analyze their abilities and interests to better match their personal needs for career development to the organization's needs. Career planning is a critical tool by which performance coaches can enhance quality, improve employee attitudes toward work, and develop greater worker satisfaction. Career-development workshops and research enable employees to learn the essentials of career planning and determine how much support the organization is willing to provide in future career development.

In career planning, you develop and provide the *means* for career awareness—selecting career-analysis instruments, helping transform performance appraisals into developmental evaluations, helping employees formulate career-development plans, and leading the transformation of the organization's culture into a developmental one. Consequently, employees and career advisors become equal partners in career awareness.

An organizational predisposition toward career planning is essential to successful career-planning programs. The career advisor, however, has an obligation to encourage as well as provide for the utilization of career planning on the part of employees.

Engaging in career-planning activities proves important for many reasons. First, such activities help organizations develop and promote employees from within. Second, most organizations have a shortage of promotable talent. Third, organizations are increasingly interested in providing career advice to their employees. Fourth, employees have expressed increasing interest in career development. Fifth, organizations are interested in increasing interest in career development and in improving their responsiveness, effectiveness, and efficiency. Sixth, organizations desire to reduce turnover and improve loyalty and productivity. Seventh, educational institutions are interested in providing a more positive recruiting image.[3] Any or all of these are excellent reasons for organizations to sponsor and encourage career-planning efforts. The result is a more talented human resource base. Ultimately, as employees improve and grow, the organization benefits.

Several obstacles inhibit the implementation of career-planning activities: (1) lack of role clarity in the organization in terms of career-planning responsibilities, (2) lack of managers skilled in career planning and related issues, and (3) the peripheral nature of career planning. These barriers indicate the need for additional evaluation by the organization; the development of a philosophy regarding career planning; an assessment of the organization's developmental procedures, including performance coaches' responsibilities; additional training; and a long-term commitment to the concept of career planning.

The challenge of career planning lies in equipping employees with necessary knowledge about self and reality. Techniques in career planning include counseling, career-planning workshops, self-development materials, occupational information, and assessment programs. Although employees are ultimately responsible for their own careers, the organization is an equal partner in career planning. Therefore, the principle purpose of career-planning activities is to encourage employees to take responsibility for their careers.

Today's career planning is a higher priority in organizations than ever before. Career advisors examine each of these forces carefully and determine the impact that each has on the organization. Once this has been achieved, performance coaches can prepare for and react to the future pressures for providing career planning.

Increasing Career Opportunities. Becoming aware of career opportunities available within an organization is the responsibility of both employees and career advisors. Employees can learn much about the history, culture, and philosophy of their organization from career advisors who are willing to share this vital information. Additionally, career advisors should identify the types of position for which the organization has the greatest need and should determine whether their employees have any interest and/or the skills necessary for upcoming positions. Career advisors arrange additional professional-development activities so that employees are able to enhance their personal competence. Moreover, career advisors communicate the type and degree of career openings presently available, along with anticipated openings and future trends.

The performance appraisal allows you to combine the roles of career advisor and performance appraiser to discuss career goals and aspirations. Simultaneously, employees should request information on the future direction of the organization and ascertain whether their personal career focus is consistent with that of the firm.

To enhance career opportunities, career advisors identify future needs of the organization and communicate them clearly to employees. You design and develop career-development and planning activities to orient employees to the organization and to stress the type of learning opportunities that are available, along with present and future career opportunities.

Responsibilities of Strategists

Strategists create long-term plans for improvement and management of employee performance; therefore, they must have the leadership and strategic competencies to design, coordinate, control, and implement planning activities. Competencies include the ability to envision, design, and communicate the big picture to all employees—which means seeing the forest in spite of the trees. Strategists demonstrate the ability to ask thought-provoking questions that help employees understand their roles and responsibilities.

Strategists must accept a variety of responsibilities. Each of these responsibilities is designed to maximize the effectiveness of performance-improvement interventions, improve communications, enhance client relationships, improve organizational performance capacity, enhance the organization's culture, and improve work environments.

Strategists interpret and impart information in order to communicate what changes in performance are needed, to help clients learn how to make needed changes, and to motivate management to accept and adopt change. It is extremely important, therefore, that you facilitate the understanding and acceptance of performance improvement and change among employees. Only then will employees be willing to implement and support performance-improvement efforts.

Strategists are responsible for supplying information on possible performance-improvement interventions, for helping employees to cope with attitudinal shifts, and for handling defensive reactions. Such activities are usually conducted during the implementation phase of the process.

Strategists help employees acquire new skills, knowledge, insights, awareness, and attitudes needed to implement change. These could include problem-solving skills, practice with giving and receiving performance feedback, listening skills, leadership development, goal setting, resolving conflicts, and diagnosing group interactions. When employees have developed such skills and knowledge, they rely less on coaches and apply what they have learned.

Strategists are also responsible for the following:

- Sponsoring performance improvement and change—Being a catalyst of performance improvement and change requires managers to build coalitions of support for performance improvement and change and to recognize others who are also committed. They enlist support from key individuals in the organization and build a responsibility matrix to bring about performance improvement and change.
- Performance landscaping—Strategists are responsible for reviewing performance throughout the organization for the purpose of making recommendations for change.
- Succession planning—These plans allows managers to identify, mold, and position replacements for key employees in the firm.
- Advocating solutions—This requires strategists to influence the organization to choose particular actions or solutions that improve performance, efficiency, and quality. Meeting this responsibility requires coaches to be very directive, proactive, and persuasive in performance-related issues. It could be said that coaches are "selling" organizational leaders during this activity.
- Futurist—As a strategist, a coach establishes a vision of the organization's future. Consequently, it is important that the strategist function

as a futurist, providing multiple options, ideas, and possibilities. The value of this activity is in the several alternatives generated for the organization.

- Solving problems—Strategists determine the root cause of problems, guaranteeing that the perceived problem is indeed the one that needs solving. Much time, effort, and money have been wasted attempting to solve "symptoms" or phantom problems instead of the true cause. A useful approach involves working with the problem as "defined" by employees in such a way that more useful definitions emerge.

Responsibilities of Performance Appraisers

Performance appraisers accept a variety of new and exciting responsibilities. Each is designed to maximize the effectiveness of employee performance and productivity. The ultimate outcome is improved organizational effectiveness.

Conduct Performance Appraisals. Coaches as performance appraisers work closely with employees during a performance appraisal. This requires creating a partnership focused on identifying the strengths and weaknesses of the employee and creating an action plan that builds on strengths, manages weaknesses, and ensures success on the job. A mutually beneficial partnership allows both parties to build a trusting, collaborative relationship that helps individuals identify performance-development opportunities. In this way, performance appraisers solicit the involvement and support of employees in their growth and development, which addresses one of the primary reasons firms fail to achieve desired performance results. We support what we create. Performance appraisers will enjoy better outcomes when employees willingly participate in their own action planning.

Performance-appraisal interviews occasionally fail to yield positive outcomes because the interviewer focuses on personal characteristics and personalities rather than performance. Another reason for disappointing outcomes involves dwelling on employees' past actions instead of focusing on future performance. Although past performance *does* provide a means of sculpting and structuring the future, a performance appraiser's attention should be on future actions and behaviors. Effective performance appraisers do the following:

- Establish appropriate performance goals and standards—Define outcomes in terms of end products or services, act as continual points of reference for settling disputes and misunderstandings about the project, and keep all objectives and associated work on track.

- Conduct developmental evaluations—Assess employees' strengths and weaknesses and analyze worker knowledge, skills, and behaviors to determine areas of excellence and those needing improvement. These evaluations present opportunities for managers and employees to discuss current and future developmental goals and objectives along with plans to achieve them, reviewing the "fit" between organizational expectations and the expectations of the employee.
- Provide feedback—Honestly discuss the employees' strengths and areas needing improvement.
- Conduct cause analysis—Cause analysis reveals the real reason or reasons that problems or gaps exist by identifying factors impeding or contributing to performance. Once a cause analysis has been completed and the true cause or causes of the performance gap have been revealed, you can develop a change intervention that addresses the root cause of the problem, thus closing the gap between the actual and desired state.
- Create plans for employee growth and development—These plans examine employee strengths, weaknesses, and areas requiring improvement, and they formulate specific action-oriented strategies for continuous improvement and success. Growth and development plans are long-term, developmental strategies (not quick fixes) mutually designed by managers and employees that are realistic, specific, attainable, and tied to a timetable (see Figure 5.4 for a sample).
- Link compensation and rewards to growth and development—Shift the focus of compensation systems such that employees are rewarded for enhancing their skills or competencies.
- Improve performance—Performance improvement focuses on problems and behaviors, not personalities. The result is desired change via positive relationships with employees, without causing hurt, anger, or defensiveness.

CONCLUSION

The roles and responsibilities of a performance coach have been identified and examined. By serving as a trainer, career advisor, strategist, or performance appraiser, the coach improves individual employee performance, which ultimately benefits the organization.

FOUR

Competencies of Performance Coaches

Obstacles or barriers to performance take many shapes, both organizationally and individually. Whether they are a result of personal or family problems, job tasks, or work environment, it is absolutely essential for performance coaches and their personnel to review barriers that might prevent performance at an acceptable level. This discussion should focus on two levels. First, considerable time should be devoted to identifying obstacles. Second, means of neutralizing, eliminating, or managing barriers require evaluation to guarantee individuals ample opportunity to perform at or above established standards.

Performance interference can be as simple as having inadequate resources to complete a job or as complicated as having competing tasks (e.g., training, report writing, meeting attendance) that prevent the job's timely execution. Regardless of their source, obstacles must be identified and overcome, particularly when they prevent employees from performing at an adequate level. Accordingly, performance coaches need a variety of competencies to be effective.

BUILDING COLLABORATIVE EMPLOYEE RELATIONSHIPS

Using the following communication techniques helps establish rapport with employees, which leads to more successful performance-improvement interventions and collaborative employee relationships. These techniques play a critical role in relating successfully with employees.

Active Listening

One of the agreed-upon keys to effective communications is listening. Good listening is an important bridge to understanding because it changes the entire relationship between you and the employee. Some 70 to 80 percent of our waking hours are spent in communication, and over half of that time involves listening. Feedback is also a necessary ingredient in effective communication and one that can be made accurate only through active listening.

The difference between active and inactive listening is the difference between truly listening and only hearing. The act of listening requires effort and concentration. Listening to employees intently helps you more readily capture content and intended meaning. Moreover, because you also convey respect through active listening, certain positive results can be predicted. That is, employees who are listened to attentively will tend to

- consider their point of view to be more important,
- state their feelings and thinking more clearly,
- listen to others more carefully when they speak,
- become less quarrelsome, and
- become more receptive to different points of view.

Developing better listening skills takes effort and dedication. Many techniques have been proven to enhance listening skills. You should do the following:

- Concentrate all your physical and mental energies on listening
- Avoid interrupting the speaker
- Demonstrate interest and alertness
- Seek an area of agreement with the employee
- Search for meaning and avoid getting hung up on specific words
- Demonstrate patience (you may be able to listen "faster" than the employee can speak)
- Provide clear and unambiguous feedback to the employee
- Repress the tendency to respond emotionally to what is said

- Ask questions when you do not understand something
- Paraphrase to ensure your understanding
- Withhold evaluation of the message until the employee is finished and you are sure you understand the message

Clarifying.   Sometimes it is helpful to make clarifying statements in an attempt to place the employee's feeling and attitudes in a clear, more recognizable form. Additionally, you may ask the employee to elaborate on a particular point or statement or to provide an example or illustration to make the meaning more clearly understood. This technique proves effective for testing understanding. Using this technique involves asking questions such as, "Are you . . . ?" "Did you . . . ?" or "How do . . . ?"

Encouraging.   This technique enables employees to continue to elaborate on their feelings and thoughts. Encouraging remarks—such as "That's understandable," "It's OK to feel that way," "That's interesting; tell me more," or "I've experienced that, too"—are useful in countering employees' feelings of inadequacy. Such responses also prompt action by encouraging the employee to continue the discussion. Nonverbal techniques such as a nod of the head or moving closer to the employee strengthen the employee's response and indicates that you are listening.

Interpreting.   When using this technique, you go beyond the employee's statement to explain cause-and-effect relationships and clarify implications. This approach enables employees to understand the full ramifications of what they are saying and generally results in a greater awareness of what is involved. Use of interpreting requires you to draw a conclusion about the employee's perception of a situation or event. Interpretation is subject to error; that is, the interpretation could be incorrect.

Interpreting provides a basis for publicly testing any assumptions made during a conversation. Thus, it allows the employee the opportunity to acknowledge the correctness of your interpretation and verify his or her point of view. Common statements—such as those that begin "If I understand correctly" and "Based on what you have said"—frame your interpretations.

Paraphrasing.   With this technique, you attempt to restate, in your own words, the employee's basic message. The primary purpose of paraphrasing is to test your understanding of what has been said. Another purpose is to communicate to the employee that you are trying to understand the basic message and, if the paraphrasing is successful, that you have been following what the employee said. An example of paraphrasing would be "You seem to be saying that his overbearing personality makes it difficult to accomplish your work."

Nonverbals.   Nonverbals make up as much as 93 percent of meaning in communications.[1] Carefully control your own body language and observe that of others. Looking into someone's eyes, nodding, and leaning forward convey interest in others and their messages. Fidgeting, crossing of the arms, and leaning back reveal lack of interest, trust, or concern.

Employees are quite aware of the nonverbal behaviors of some managers and often avoid certain topics and discussions as a result. Nonverbal communication is also important in establishing and maintaining an environment that is conducive to sharing. In fact, this might even lead an employee to avoid contact with some managers. A simple nonverbal technique such as proper eye contact can greatly improve the communication between you and your employee.

Knowledge of Positive Work Environment

A closer examination reveals that certain key elements are needed for development of a nonthreatening, comfortable, and conducive-to-sharing work environment. These components are essential to your success and include attentiveness, empathy, genuineness, understanding, acceptance, and involvement.

Attentiveness.   Too many managers cannot wait until an employee stops speaking so that they can present their own point of view. Attentiveness refers to the effort made by you to hear the message conveyed by employees. It requires skills in listening and observing. Inattentiveness communicates a lack of respect and diminishes the importance of the employee's ideas. Conversely, listening conveys to employees that you are interested in and sensitive to their feelings and thoughts.

Empathy.   When you have the ability to feel and describe the thoughts and feelings of others, you are considered empathetic. Commonly, being empathetic has been described as putting yourself in the other person's shoes, attempting, in other words, to see things from another person's vantage point. Empathetic understanding is the ability to understand, recognize, and sense the feelings that another person reveals through his or her behavioral and verbal expressions. It is not enough to understand the behavior or feelings of employees; you must also communicate that understanding to them. True empathy is an active event rather than a passive one.

Genuineness. Genuineness is demonstrated when you know your true feelings, act on them, and communicate them when necessary. Genuineness implies being honest and candid with yourself and others and not pretending to be something you are not. Genuineness refers to your ability to be yourself in all situations rather than play a part or role. Self-disclosure is invaluable, yet does not mean that you should totally unveil your personal and private life. Employees want to believe in you.

Understanding. Although no one fully understands his or her employees, it can be said that the path to understanding is essentially a process of sharing. Understanding is recognizing and correctly interpreting the feelings, thoughts, and behaviors of another person. Employees express themselves through verbal and nonverbal language; your challenge is to interpret and provide clarity for you both.

Understanding can he characterized as internal or external. Internal understanding refers to your ability to step into the perceptual world of your employees. This is done in an effort to discover *their* internal world—their fears, successes, and failures. It is at this level that genuine communication begins. External understanding refers to an awareness of employees' behavior and actions on your part. This means being able to identify the explicit actions of employees and account for results.

Acceptance. Acceptance is the basic attitude that you should hold toward an employee, and it requires respect for the employee as a person of worth. Coaches demonstrate acceptance through willingness to allow employees to differ from one another. This willingness is based on the belief that each employee is a complex being made up of different experiences, values, and attitudes. Acceptance has been defined as a warm regard for an individual as a person of unconditional self-worth and an acceptance of and a regard for his or her attitudes, no matter how negative or positive.[2]

Involvement. Although acceptance and understanding are passive, involvement implies action; it means active participation in the employees' problems and needs. Therefore, a willingness to care and feel responsible for the other person is rightly called involvement. Only active participants become agents for change, engaging in activities that allow face-to-face contact with employees. Training activities demonstrate the interest that you have in your employees.

COMPETENCIES OF TRAINERS

Instructional Competencies

A primary activity of trainers is instruction. This means facilitating learning activities as well as conducting on-the-job training. Trainers use various methods of instruction. Examples include behavior modeling, simulations and games, demonstrations, discussion, lecture, and small-group techniques. On-the-job training activities are informal (unstructured) or formal (structured). Informal sessions occur daily in organizations, such as when a performance coach provides simple job-related information in a nonstructured, matter-of-fact manner. For example, a manager tells a new employee in a fast-food restaurant how to greet customers. The information shared is not a part of formal training required by the organization, yet is based on the insight and experience of the manager. This information may or may not be shared with all employees because it is a spur-of-the-moment shared activity, conducted to help the new employee learn the tricks of the trade. Conversely, formal, structured, on-the-job training activities are offered to all employees equally in order to provide continuity. These activities are designed to provide the correct or exact procedures for completing a particular job. Formal activities tend to be quite detailed, requiring many hours to prepare and complete. They are considered structured because a proper order is required, and they are often sequenced with other training activities. Formal training typically includes learning objectives and activities designed to bring about appropriate behaviors, skills, or competencies. To provide realism, they are often conducted at the workstation or job site. This gives employees a chance to practice job skills and receive immediate feedback on performance.

As instructors, some performances coaches train other managers in how to train their employees. This important activity, often overlooked, significantly impacts the organization and its employees, as more people get involved in the individual development function.

In 1988, the International Board of Standards for Training, Performance and Instruction (IBSTPI) published a list of 14 competencies for instructors. Known as *The Standards*, the list provides instructors and their organizations with criteria for developing learning programs. The criteria serve as a means for measuring the current skill levels of instructors as well as learners' performance. They represent the most comprehensive listing of competencies yet published for instructors in the workplace; the criteria are as follows:

1. Analyze course materials and learner information.
2. Assure preparation of the instructional site.
3. Establish and maintain instructor credibility.
4. Manage the learning environment.
5. Demonstrate effective communication skills.
6. Demonstrate effective presentation skills.
7. Demonstrate effective questioning skills and techniques.
8. Respond appropriately to learners' needs for clarification or feedback.
9. Provide reinforcement and motivational incentives.
10. Use instructional methods appropriately.
11. Use media effectively.
12. Evaluate learner performance.
13. Evaluate instruction.
14. Report evaluation information.

Knowledge of the Principles of Adult Learning

Trainers apply four fundamental principles of adult learning when working with employees. They are as follows:

1. Theory should be linked with practical application to reduce resistance to learning such material. In other words, present new information only if it is meaningful and practical.
2. Adults maintain the ability to learn throughout their lifetime and should be treated accordingly. Present information in a manner that permits mastery yet takes into account gradual declines in eyesight and hearing.
3. Present only one idea or concept at a time to help adults integrate it with their existing knowledge. Minimize competing intellectual demands in an effort to increase comprehension. The principal goal of learning activities is the development of knowledge, skills, competencies, and attitudes that help adults in the successful resolution of existing problems and improved performance. Therefore, the issue is not which method to use or how rigorous the process, but simply the development of the desired competencies, skills, knowledge, and attitudes.

4. Use feedback and frequent summarization to augment retention and recall. Unfortunately, these activities are often overlooked or greatly deemphasized because of the lack of time available for learning. However, failure to incorporate feedback and summaries into learning could result in incorrect application of the material or a failure to apply it.

Several additional underlying principles help us understand how adults learn. They include the following:

1. A supportive learning environment improves learning.
2. Learning must be properly timed.
3. Learning is a self-activity.
4. People learn at different rates.
5. Positive reinforcement enhances learning.
6. People learn best by doing.
7. "Whole-part-whole" learning is best.
8. Learning is continuous and a continual process.
9. Learning results from stimulation of the senses.

Several useful characteristics of adults can be maximized when trainers deliver or facilitate learning activities. For example, adult learners have ideas to contribute and a good deal of firsthand experience that should be tapped during training. Adult learners have set habits and strong opinions, which affect learning. Adult learners have very tangible things to lose in a learning setting (e.g., reputation, respect) and are supposed to appear in control, and therefore, they display restricted emotional responses. They have a great many preoccupations outside a practical learning situation that negatively impact learning. Adult learners have developed group behavior consistent with their needs and have established rational frameworks consisting of values, attitudes, and tendencies.

Many adult learners have developed selective and critical "stimuli filters" and thus have strong feelings about learning situations, some positive and some negative. Commonly, adult learners resist authority and autocratic instruction yet respond positively to reinforcement and encouragement. Adult learners need a purpose for participating in learning activities but can change their outlook when presented with a compelling reason for involvement. Finally, adult learners have a past that can positively influence learning. All of these factors should be considered and incorporated into learning situations in order to enhance and improve learning.

Understanding Adults as Learners

For some time, educational research has documented that adults learn in a variety of ways. Most commonly, the primary learning style of adults is interactive (kinesthetic). Surprisingly, oral and print media receive low to middle rankings for adult learning preference. Additionally, most adults seek out learning experiences in order to cope with specific life-changing events, and they are certain to engage actively in any learning that promises to help. The theory of andragogy maintains that adults want to participate actively in the assessment of their own needs and in planning their own learning activities.[3] Adults, therefore, want to establish their learning goals and objectives, as well as participate in evaluating their learning.

Adult learners want to immediately apply what they have learned. This is especially true when a person is attempting to adjust to new responsibilities that come with promotion or transfer. Therefore, timely learning is extremely important to adult learners. Avoid using lectures or readings; neither one is the most appropriate or preferred learning styles for adults. Unfortunately, many learning activities take place because the organization deems them necessary (e.g., to "fix" broken employees) or important—not because the needs of employees demand them. This is contrary to andragogy's basic assumption that adult learners want to participate actively in their own learning.

Summarizing Skills

Summarizing conveys to learners the essence of what has been said throughout an information exchange. You may wish to ask employees to agree or disagree with your summary in order to make certain that all concepts are understood. An example of a summarizing statement is "Let me take a moment to summarize our discussion. . . . " Summarizing techniques encompass several thoughts and concepts that frame the most appropriate steps to follow for each employee. Alternatively, trainers may wish to have employees summarize the discussion, which provides another check for accuracy and understanding.

Questioning Skills

Questioning is a common, yet often overused, communication technique. Questions should be used only to direct the conversation into more constructive and informative channels or to obtain specifically needed information. Questions may be directed at an entire group or a specific employee. Questions remain powerful tools with which to facilitate group discussion, guide the flow and direction of conversation, and help you obtain specific information very quickly.

Two types of questions prove useful: open- and closed-ended. Open-ended questions encourage respondents to expand on the topic. These questions help employees widen their perceptual field and prepare them to consider divergent points of view. Quite simply, open-ended questions open the doors to developing a positive relationship and good rapport. An open-ended question is less threatening to employees and allows them to convey their points of view. An example might be "How do you feel about the effectiveness of the new performance appraisal program?" Employees answering this type of question may reveal different opinions.

In contrast, closed-ended questions can be answered in relatively few words and have specific responses. They are important in guiding the conversation and for gathering essential information quickly. Examples of a closed-ended question might be "How long have you been in your current position?" or "Is this a problem you'd like to solve?" This type of question ignores response effectiveness and employee feelings in favor of gathering needed information quickly.

COMPETENCIES OF CAREER ADVISORS

Career advisors exhibit competencies that include collaborating, diagnosing, reality testing, goal setting, and motivating to action. Each competency requires mastery of related supporting skills, as described in the following lists.

Collaborating

- Establishing open communication with employees
- Encouraging employees to share insights or the results of their self-assessments
- Listening rather than talking
- Questioning to understand an individual's values, interests, skills, and needs
- Identifying additional needs that employees may have
- Focusing on the issues important to the employee

Diagnosing

- Dealing with emotional issues and providing support before addressing career issues
- Withholding judgment of the problem until it is clearly diagnosed
- Forming a hypothesis about the problem and using appropriate questioning techniques to identify the real issues
- Remaining objective and not acting on personal biases

Reality Testing

- Maintaining a developmental approach as opposed to an evaluative one
- Helping employees understand how present performance affects future opportunities
- Defining strengths, weaknesses, and developmental needs
- Helping employees recognize the importance of their reputation
- Assessing the viability of goals and action plans
- Providing support and questioning as needed

Goal Setting

- Helping individuals define viable career goals based on their preliminary assessment and planning
- Helping employees write specific, measurable, positive goals
- Analyzing employees' goals to determine action steps
- Providing reality testing when goals are unrealistic

Motivating to Action

- Determining developmental actions to help employees reach their goals
- Completing a written development plan as a communication tool, a working document, and a record of developmental actions
- Identifying barriers and figuring out ways to overcome them
- Offering encouragement and prodding to keep employees moving ahead
- Celebrating successes

Employee Relationship–Building Skills

Career advisors support and nurture others, particularly during periods of conflict and stress. This skill is critical just before and during change initiatives, and it builds rapport with employees.

Interpersonal Skills. At the heart of the career advisor–employee relationship are interpersonal skills. When performance coaches serve as career advisors, they demonstrate respect for the personal boundaries and values of their employees via interpersonal skills such as active listening and questioning. Interpersonal skills structure the communication process between coaches and their employees, promoting acceptance and positive regard. The ability to listen well and empathize is especially important during interviews, in conflict situations, and when constituent stress is high. Finally, via interpersonal skills, performance coaches create a working relationship and an environment in which employees feel safe and secure. Consequently, employees are more willing to try new and unfamiliar techniques, technologies, and so forth.

Silence. Silence definitely can be golden. This competency is much more difficult to master than it seems. The use of silence enables employees to think through what has transpired, gather their thoughts, and provide additional information or explanation if appropriate or needed. It is important to remember that even experienced career advisors are initially uncomfortable with silence as a technique. With practice, however, it becomes apparent that intentional silence provides employees with additional time to explore their feelings more deeply and to think about what they are going to say. Silence, unfortunately, can be abused; more than a minute of silence, for example, often causes discomfort. Thus, avoid extensive periods of silence because they may be misinterpreted and perceived as unresponsiveness. Silence is most useful when used in combination with other techniques, such as encouraging and active listening.

Reflecting. Reflection helps career advisors guide the conversation and bring out into the open feelings and hidden agendas. This is important because deeply hidden feelings can affect virtually every thought or behavior of an employee. These feelings often hinder the exchange process between you and your employees and thus need to be brought to the surface to be dealt with effectively. This helps develop an open and honest exchange between you and your employees.

Reflecting allows career advisors to surface and verbalize the emotional or substantive content of the employee's words. Its purpose is to reveal that you understand correctly what the employee is feeling, thinking, or experiencing. It may actually verbalize the core of the employee's attitudes when he or she has trouble articulating. An example of a summarizing statement would be "So you're looking for a training program to help you develop interpersonal skills to improve your effectiveness as a supervisor?"

Tentative Analysis. Tentative analysis is a "hunch" interpretation that is usually narrow in scope of possibilities. Because of its tentative nature, this analysis is usually stated in the form of a question. As such, it is a form of short summarization. Tentative analysis stops short of being conclusive because it generally deals with one thought or concept instead of several. Its chief advantage is the way it communicates that you are attempting to test publicly an employee's understanding of his or her thoughts and ideas. By doing this one step at a time, you demonstrate patience with and respect for the employee's viewpoint. An example of tentative analysis would be "I have a feeling you're not very satisfied with the quality of the sales training program. Is that correct?"

These techniques enable career advisors to develop a comfortable working relationship with employees—one conducive to sharing ideas and feelings. Such a relationship is essential to the development of rapport with employees.

COMPETENCIES OF STRATEGISTS

As a strategist, a performance coach demonstrates insight into the operational business aspects of organizational systems. This insight includes knowledge of business fundamentals as they apply to organizations, systems theory, organizational culture, and politics. Strategists demonstrate their understanding of stakeholders' needs and expectations along with financial and business issues facing their firm.

Organizational Development Competencies

Strategists rely on a set of guiding principles to direct their behavior and anchor them during difficult times. Consequently, they acquire problem-solving, conceptual, research, and analytical skills in order to become effective in managing and implementing organizational change. They respond to unforeseen contingencies, provide appropriate solutions to complex and sensitive issues, and conduct a wide variety of activities designed to enhance performance.

Strategists identify possible performance-improvement interventions, apply them at the individual or group levels, and decide when training—or other learning activities—are most appropriate to close performance gaps. All of these situations require significant skills that include conceptual, technical, integrative, analytical, and specialized knowledge.

Conceptual Skills.   Conceptual skills helps strategists analyze performance problems, implement performance-improvement interventions, and evaluate their effectiveness. These skills allow you to create a framework to guide your behavior—one that you use continuously to test solutions and recommendations. Such a framework should also be used when conducting organizational analysis and performance-improvement interventions and when evaluating outcomes.

Technical Skills.   A strategist's skill set entails forecasting, data gathering, analysis, solution generation, planning, implementation, and evaluation. These technical skills are used to analyze and evaluate change interventions and develop new initiatives to meet specific employee needs. A commonly forgotten technical skill is the ability to respond to unforeseen contingencies.

Integrative Skills.   When strategists use interpersonal, conceptual, and technical skills together to manage projects, integrative skills are required. Integrative skills require you to identify the components of a problem, define their interrelationships, and then fashion interventions that improve performance. Integrative skills link ideas, concepts, and strategies resulting in dynamic, innovative approaches to problem solving.

Objectivity.   Effective strategists possess the ability to remain impartial regardless of their personal values and biases and in spite of an organization's culture, traditions, and vested interests. This ability is commonly referred to as objectivity. Objectivity is often difficult, however, for the coach to master because of his or her perspectives and knowledge of the organization. Remaining objective enables performance coaches to function as the social conscience of the organization and is, perhaps, the greatest single benefit of the strategist role.

Specialized Knowledge.   Coaches possess a unique set of skills and specialized knowledge. Performance coaches need depth of understanding to be successful and must maintain a unique set of skills or specialized knowledge in performance management and organizational development.

Organizational Competencies

Strategists improve their organizational impact and influence by demonstrating organizational understanding, political awareness, and organizational awareness.

Business Understanding.   An awareness of how organizations work is essential for strategists and enables them to think like their employees. Once understood, knowledge of systems theory, culture, and politics provides coaches with a better understanding of the organization. With the knowledge of how things get done and how decisions are made inside a firm, strategists are better able to facilitate change without disrupting the organization's operations.

Strategists add value to their organizations by understanding daily operations, which helps them adapt their practices and activities to ever-changing conditions. Although strategists may be experts in learning, performance, and change initiatives, these skills will be of little value to the organization unless they are able to adapt their practices to changing conditions and circumstances. Consequently, strategists gain experience in functional areas such as finance, operations, or budgeting to generate pertinent, practical solutions for their employees. Effective strategists also demonstrate organizational understanding via knowledge of constituent needs and expectations. This knowledge enables them to adapt their practices, procedures, products, innovations, and services, which allows them to better serve their employees.

Political Awareness. Regardless of its size and complexity, an organization has a political structure, work environment, and culture that influence its decisions and behavior and that impact stability and continuity. These components are often a major reason that organizations experience difficulties. When strategists are unable to convince organization leaders that their firm is dysfunctional, an objective third-party change agent (internal or external) may be needed to become the formal representative of change.

Organizational Awareness. As a strategist, your understanding of organizational operations enables you to promote needed performance improvement. This knowledge aids in identifying organizational needs, selecting solutions, implementing interventions, and evaluating the results of a performance-improvement intervention. Knowing where to go for information, insight, and recommendations helps strategists avoid the pitfalls common in organizational life. Another benefit of organizational awareness is a better understanding of the organization's political structure and decision-making procedures. These are critical in gaining the support needed to implement meaningful change.

Consulting Skills. As strategists work through the steps of the performance improvement and management model (see chapter 6), they rely on consulting skills. This includes maintaining contact with the employee, communicating when appropriate, negotiating any changes in the performance-improvement process, providing support and maintenance as required, and terminating the engagement.

Consulting is a synergistic process in which the expertise of both the employee and the consultant is maximized. In essence, the whole is greater than the sum of the parts—which epitomizes the synergistic consulting process. Strategists, therefore, develop skills that enable them to enter into discussions with employees, determine their needs, identify performance requirements and results, and formulate action plans.

Partnering Skills.   Strategists take the initiative to meet, work with, and gain the trust of other organizational leaders. Forging partnerships with executives, senior managers, other managers, and subject-matter experts is one way of achieving this goal. Developing a comprehensive network is another way of forming partnerships. Networking involves identifying people throughout the organization, in various positions and levels, with whom ongoing contact would be mutually beneficial. Members of the network provide strategists with information regarding departmental objectives, initiatives, career opportunities, strategic plans, and employee attitudes, morale, and concerns.

System Thinking Skills.   Identifying, analyzing, and evaluating systems within an organization are essential parts of performance coaching. These tasks require the ability to assess elements of the organizational system that are related to one another and determine which inputs, processes, and outputs from one element of a system interact with other elements of that system. Strategists predict which parts of the organizational system are likely to change when another part of the system changes, and they use the performance improvement and management framework to manage these changes.

Project Management Skills.   Every performance-improvement and performance-management intervention is a project. Planning a project requires a comprehensive and complex set of skills that should not be underestimated. Such an intervention has many facets. As such, strategists need skills in project management to lead such projects from beginning to end. Project management skills overlap with the skills required for consulting and change management, in that strategists assess the relationship that they have with an employee and adjust the improvement and management intervention accordingly. They also analyze risks to project completion and engage in contingency planning to minimize those risks. Strategists manage the entire project to guarantee that its requirements are being fulfilled.

Change Management Skills.   Every time performance improves, a change has occurred that represents a new way of working. For some employees, the change may be insignificant, whereas for others it may be quite drastic. To deal with resistance to change and to foster an environment that is conducive to change, strategists enlist the support and cooperation of employees and others involved with the change. Strategists recognize the stages of change and employ the appropriate strategies for each stage.

Teamwork Skills. Performance improvement and management interventions are often complex, requiring strategists to possess knowledge of teamwork and team-building skills. These competencies includes planning, directing, coordinating, and managing team performance. Activities include implementing the necessary communication processes, managing meetings, identifying roles and responsibilities clearly, scheduling performance activities, identifying performance standards, sequencing complex resources, accounting for interdependencies, dividing the work into manageable units, and assigning work (see Figure 6.1).

COMPETENCIES OF PERFORMANCE APPRAISERS

The principal competencies of a performance appraiser include conflict resolution, feedback skills, and confronting skills. Conducting effective performance appraisals that are developmental, however, requires additional competencies such as analytical skills and intuition.

Conflict-Resolution Skills

Conflicting goals, ideas, policies, and practices make it almost impossible to implement meaningful change. Performance appraisers' mastery of conflict-resolution skills allows them to guide employees through the change process in a way that minimizes resistance. Conflict-resolution skills enable you to understand why resistance occurs and how to respond accordingly, to maintain an objective viewpoint, and to demonstrate fairness. Such insight is advantageous in overcoming resistance to change.

Feedback Skills

Managerial malpractice occurs most frequently when managers fail to provide appropriate performance feedback to their employees. Some managers mistakenly believe that their employees know when they are or are not performing correctly. Unfortunately, many do not. It is your responsibility to provide clear, concise, sincere, and timely feedback. Here is a good working definition of feedback: getting timely and specific information about job performance that includes praise or developmental direction. *Timely* means giving feedback on a continuous basis, not just during annual performance reviews. *Specific* implies documenting exact performance behaviors that can be referenced when giving feedback to an employee. *Praise* and *developmental direction* entail providing feedback that relates to entire job performance. These definitions help entrench a performance coach's feedback philosophy.

Performance feedback can be verbal or written, solicited or unsolicited, direct or indirect, and friendly or unfriendly. Feedback is critical to enhancing employee growth and development because they cannot perform adequately unless they understand how they are doing. Managers must help employees know when they are producing the kind of performance outcomes needed by the organization or completing performance activities correctly.

Providing performance feedback helps managers build synergistic relationships with their employees while reducing conflicts regarding performance. Feedback is a powerful motivator and source of encouragement for employees and helps them better understand their strengths and weaknesses so that a development plan can be created. Giving timely and specific feedback leads to improved business results. Finally, the ability to confront difficult issues is essential for performance appraisers because much of their work consists of exposing issues that employees are reluctant to address.

Implementing Performance Feedback. Performance appraisers communicate feedback in a way that encourages employees to improve their performance. Feedback should be delivered positively, which prevents employees from becoming defensive. It should not be a surprise but be ongoing. In other words, performance feedback should reinforce things that employees know about themselves and quickly recognize so that they may make minor corrections in their job performance.

Prior to sharing your observations with employees, prepare appropriate and adequate documentation. In other words, leave a paper trail. Although recording every incident of an employee's performance is unrealistic, observable patterns of poor or good performance should be noted. Thorough documentation of poor performance assures objectivity in dealing with the problem and the employee. Precise, comprehensive documentation will place you on firm legal footing if an employee's performance leads to termination.

An eight-step process may be used by performance appraisers to provide their employees with feedback regarding incorrect performance:

1. Clarify the performance problem by telling the employee exactly what was done incorrectly and provide feedback immediately.

2. Allow the employee to react and respond to feedback; listen to the employee's response and observe his or her nonverbal behavior.
3. Offer concrete evidence of the poor performance to increase understanding of the problem.
4. Identify the strengths possessed by the employee that may compensate for the weakness in performance.
5. Identify the appropriate performance that the employee can demonstrate, including exact steps to be followed, changes to be made, or the way to go about improving or ensuring quality.
6. Identify ways of improving performance or the skills or knowledge necessary for improvement.
7. Review the consequences of continuous poor performance (e.g., discipline, suspension, termination, and so on) because it is your responsibility to make certain the employee understands that poor performance will not be acceptable and that change must be forthcoming.
8. Be certain that the employee understands it is his or her responsibility to correct performance and that the employee has ownership of the problem.

Confronting Skills

Many managers have difficulty confronting employees who perform poorly. Some avoid confrontation, hoping it will somehow work itself out, whereas others become overly aggressive, making it personal. As a result, emotions explode, feelings are hurt, accusations are made, and everyone feels resentment. Furthermore, performance does not improve. The outcomes are strained relationships with employees and a loss of credibility on the part of managers. Successfully mastering confronting skills, therefore, enables you to avoid these pitfalls.

When confronting employees regarding their performance, coaches demonstrate aggressive, submissive, or assertive behavior.

Aggressive Behavior. Aggressive managers get things done by being abusive, rude, or sarcastic. They express their feelings, needs, and ideas at the expense of their employees, and they dominate employees or insist on having the final word on topics of conversation. Aggressive managers tend to have little interest in what is important to their employees, which forces some to subvert or undermine coworkers' loyalty and dedication.

Submissive Behavior. Submissive managers do not express their honest feelings, needs, values, or concerns. Often, they let their employees dictate the level and quality of performance. Behaviors such as shrugging of the shoulders, lack of eye contact, an excessively soft voice, and hesitant speech demonstrate an apologetic approach that prevents managers from being taken seriously. Submissive managers allow employees to violate them by denying them their managerial rights and ignoring their requests. Consequently, their desires and needs are not fulfilled by their employees.

Assertive Behavior. Assertive managers express their needs, values, concerns, and ideas in direct and appropriate ways and stand up for their rights—without abusing or dominating their employees. They do not violate the needs of their employees while meeting their own needs.

True assertiveness is a way of behaving that confirms your personal worth and dignity while simultaneously confirming and maintaining the worth and dignity of your employees.

Confrontation is not necessarily criticism. However, performance appraisers must remain positive for confrontations to be successful. They need to (1) learn to communicate specifically what behaviors or performance must improve, (2) focus on the performance problem rather than the person, (3) use confrontation to produce the desired change without causing the employee to become defensive, and (4) maintain a positive relationship with employees.

Mastering the art of confrontation requires development of three critical sets of skills, each of which helps the performance appraiser improve employee performance while maintaining positive interpersonal relationships:

1. Assertion skills: These verbal and nonverbal skills enable you to maintain respect, satisfy employees' needs, and defend employees' rights without manipulating, dominating, or controlling them.
2. Conflict-resolution skills: Such skills allow you to deal with the emotional turbulence that typically accompanies conflict.
3. Collaborative problem-solving skills: These skills include ways of resolving conflicts to everyone's satisfaction.

The greatest benefits to the organization can be realized through a performance appraiser's use of confronting skills. Here your entire attention is focused on improving performance and resolving problems. These improvements can help the organization become more competitive in the marketplace, which increases market share and leads to greater profitability.

Other Performance-Appraiser Competencies

Analytical Skills. It is a performance coach's responsibility to know how to generate information; analyze it; distinguish among problems, symptoms, and causes; identify solutions to problems; and recommend appropriate solutions. Such experience is gained by dealing with difficult situations within an organization and requires advanced analytical skills.

Intuition. Performance coaches should have the ability to recognize their own feelings and intuitions quickly.[4] This is important in order to distinguish the coach's own perceptions from those of the constituent, and these feelings and intuitions can then be used as interventions when appropriate and timely.

CONCLUSION

At trainers, career advisors, strategists, and performance appraisers, coaches employ a myriad of skills. Successful coaching includes knowledge and execution of communications, knowledge of adult learning, and interpersonal, conceptual, technical, integrative, political, consulting, project-management, team-building, change, and feedback skills. Each unique role demands expertise in specific competencies.

FIVE

The Performance Coaching and Management Process

The performance challenge facing every organization is to develop management systems that make employees the organization's greatest asset. Designing, developing, and implementing an organization-wide performance-management process links performance to the organization's strategic goals and objectives, employee needs and expectations, and employee compensation and rewards. Applying the concepts, principles, and ideas of the performance-management process at both the organizational and individual levels promotes maximum efficiency and performance throughout the organization.

Many ineffective organizations use an outdated, overly simple performance-management process in which (1) they identify and assemble the material resources required for employees to perform the job, (2) workers engage in activities to complete tasks, and (3) managers assess employees' performance and allocate compensation and rewards. This simple process has its roots in the industrial revolution of more than a hundred years ago, when supervisors needed a fast, efficient way to manage a multitude of workers often performing similar routine manufacturing tasks. Today's sophisticated workforce demands more of its managers.

The dilemma facing many organizations is their ignorance regarding how to manage performance, develop people, or create initiatives and techniques that enhance effectiveness. Quite simply, organizations must transform their employees into high performers who are their greatest asset. This requires creating a performance-management system that allows organizations to prepare for growth, achieve their strategic goals and objectives, and enhance organizational capability and competitiveness.

Successful performance-management initiatives mandate significant change in an organization's performance-improvement philosophy, operations, and strategy. This monumental effort requires performance coaches to sponsor and embrace change, given that they are responsible for the performance of their organization and its members.

PRINCIPLES OF PERFORMANCE IMPROVEMENT

Why do employees behave the way they do, sometimes failing to achieve the performance results required of them? Three fundamental principles explain most behaviors and why organizations fail to secure the results they desire. These principles include performance–reward disconnect, performance confusion, and inspection failure.

Many employees fail to perform adequately because there is no correlation between their performance and what is rewarded by the organization (performance–reward disconnect). Some organizations, for example, embrace the concept of team building and invest much time and money training their people in the skills, knowledge, and practice of self-directed work teams; however, they continue to compensate their employees for individual performance. Thus, performance behaviors that an organization desires are ignored or punished in the workplace.

Organizations send mixed messages by demanding quality work yet establishing unrealistic deadlines for completion; expecting projects to be finished on time, but doing nothing when a manager delays until the last minute to begin; or rewarding those employees who look the busiest or work the longest hours, while emphasizing other results such as speed or efficiency. Improving performance requires a direct correlation between desired performance and rewards. Individuals rewarded for the right performance will continue to produce similarly, as will those rewarded for improper behavior.

Inappropriate performance also occurs when managers fail to communicate which results are the most important or when they treat all performance results the same. We refer to this as performance confusion because the behavior confuses employees and causes them to prioritize results according to their own perspectives, which may or may not align with organizational expectations. The problem, however, is not with employee performance, but with managers' inability to prioritize performance outcomes and communicate these to employees. Correction requires you to determine and convey which results are truly important and which are less so. These priorities must be communicated to employees and rewarded accordingly.

Occasionally, managers neglect to inspect their employees' work (inspection failure). When little time is spent reviewing or inspecting employees' outputs, they are on their own to produce results they perceive to be important to the organization. Effective performance coaches link expectations with inspection, which can occur during performance coaching or developmental evaluations. Employees must know what is important and that their performance coaches will be inspecting performance outputs.

BENEFITS OF PERFORMANCE MANAGEMENT

In reality, performance management is everyone's responsibility—and everyone benefits. The benefits of performance management are numerous for employees, management, and the organization.

For employees, performance management motivates employees who take responsibility for their own development while eliminating unrealistic career expectations, particularly when organizations face cutbacks, flattening, or reorganization. It helps employees understand the urgency of keeping skills and abilities current, creates meaningful growth and development plans, and increases involvement in decision making.

For managers, performance management encourages leaders and managers to support continuous learning and development, helps supervisors and managers develop their employees, and enhances the managers' interpersonal relationship skills. It helps supervisors match organizational realities to recruiting promises and cultivates flexible employees capable of moving out of narrowly defined tasks and into functional roles. Finally, it develops specific performance goals and objectives for their staff in support of organizational strategy.

For organizations, performance management reduces turnover of highly skilled employees by providing environments conducive to growth and development. It assists in human resource planning, enhances organizational responsiveness and competitiveness through productive, motivated employees, and increases commitment from employees at all levels. Finally, it improves individual performance that contributes to the greater good.

THE PERFORMANCE COACHING
AND MANAGEMENT PROCESS

Although not every performance problem requires endless examination of all possibilities, they do necessitate exploration of each performance problem in relation to the mission of the organization, which links actions to a context for improvement. Thus, the performance coaching and management process approach blends the entire performance management process into one cohesive system (see Figure 5.1). It links job design and analysis, human resource planning, resources, individual and organizational goals and objectives, performance execution, performance appraisal, growth and development planning, and compensation and rewards to the process of improving employee self-esteem, career satisfaction, and motivation, thus serving as a process for engineering performance.

Performance models such as the performance coaching and management process define performance that is causally linked to accomplishment of business goals. The business goals of the organization are the targets to which performance models are directed. Furthermore, it is critical for you to fully comprehend the organization's business goals. Without this understanding, you risk developing inaccurate or incomplete approaches to performance improvement.

One of the primary purposes of the performance coaching and management process is to provide a roadmap to continuously develop and improve the organization's performance. In this way, organizational effectiveness can be enhanced on an ongoing basis.

Job Design and Analysis

An important and often overused and misunderstood element of performance management is the job description—because it seldom clearly communicates the link between performance outputs, performance activities, performance standards, and the competencies to perform a job correctly. Typically, job descriptions illustrate the most appropriate competencies required to execute a job, yet fail to identify the performance standards that determine when performance activities and outputs are generated at an acceptable level.

Effective job descriptions are written to achieve four goals:

1. Clearly identify performance outputs for each job
2. Isolate the performance activities required by employees to produce these deliverables

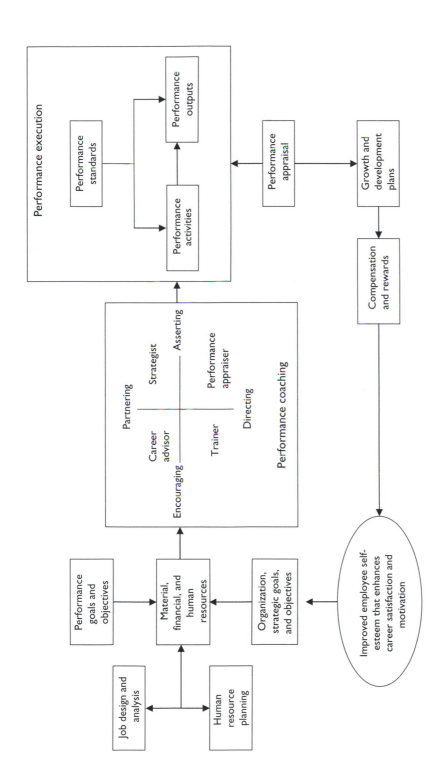

Figure 5.1 The Performance Coaching and Management Process

3. Demonstrate the relationship between activities and outputs
4. Highlight the performance standards required for activities and deliverables

Quite simply, a job description is a written document that describes an employee's performance activities and deliverables, along with the corresponding standards. Reshaping, redefining, replacing, reorganizing, or improving job design may be in order when organizations fail to achieve their sales revenue, market share, or profitability goals.

Job design is defined as the series of steps used in producing a product or service. Jobs that fail to help an organization achieve its strategic business goals and objectives cease to be valuable. It is extremely important, therefore, to link all job-design activities to these goals and objectives. The first step in the job-design process is job analysis, which identifies requirements for a specific job classification within the organization. Job analysis reveals the relationships among jobs; enhances career planning; forecasts human resource needs; identifies training, transfer, and promotion requirements; evaluates employee performance; and involves compensation reviews. Job analysis allows organizations to establish important elements of a performance-management system, including

- creating job classifications useful in developing selection requirements,
- providing training and developing feedback and motivation systems,
- creating performance-appraisal systems, and
- developing compensation systems.

Job analysis identifies what people do and how and why they do it, which provides information for selecting, appraising, developing, compensating, and disciplining employees. Job analysis reveals barriers to successful performance, determines learning needs for new and experienced employees, frames realistic performance standards, and illustrates how employee work activities contribute to achieving organizational objectives. Job analysis is useful in uncovering opportunities for performance improvement and employee growth and development. A typical job analysis reveals five interrelated components: performance outputs, performance activities, job descriptions, performance standards, and competency maps.

The term *performance outputs* refers to accomplishments—the hourly, daily, weekly, monthly, quarterly, or yearly production of employees in a specific job classification.[1] They are the tangibles and intangibles employees are paid to produce (e.g., the number of successful sales calls made by telemarketing representatives, the number of sales made per month by sales personnel, service claims handled by customer service representatives, and so on). They are also the deliverables that employees are paid to produce both internally and externally. Internally focused performance outputs consist of deliverables used by other employees in the execution of their jobs, typically when producing deliverables intended for the marketplace. External deliverables are those products or services made available to consumers outside the organization.

Performance activities are the actions in which employees engage in the creation of performance outputs. They are the small steps employees take to complete a job. These include microtasks, which collectively form the steps in an employee's job. For example, all jobs include a series of performance activities that, when used in combination, generate the desired performance deliverables.

Performance standards are the targets used to measure the quality of employee performance outputs and the efficiency of their performance activities. Performance standards represent two distinctly different measurement criteria: (1) to identify the excellence factors needed in assessing quality of products and services and to (2) identify best practices. Performance standards serve as targets for employees when generating performance outputs or executing performance activities. They are extremely important when improving both effectiveness and efficiency. Without performance standards, employees have no idea whether they are creating outputs or executing activities acceptable to internal or external stakeholders.

A performer's *competency map* is the last component of the job design. Competency maps can be quite complex because they reflect all the knowledge, skills, and appropriate attitudes employees must possess to adequately complete performance activities used in generating performance outputs. These maps can also be used to determine the training and development activities in which employees must participate to master performance.

Thorough analysis of the job's tasks, requirements, and goals allows identification of the knowledge, skills, and competencies employees need in order to be successful in the position. Therefore, competency maps are useful in recruiting and selecting qualified applicants for given position classifications, in determining the growth and development activities in which employees must participate to master performance, and in revealing individual strengths and weaknesses. In short, competency maps are an evaluation tool useful in determining employee strengths and weaknesses, thereby serving as a template for formulating performance growth and development plans.

Human Resource Planning

How do organizations produce successful results? Simple. They have a plan for having the right people in the right place at the right time.

Therefore, the first step of the performance coaching and management process involves identifying the human resources needed to accomplish the work. This requires one of the most complex organizational planning activities, which is known as human resource (HR) planning. Human resource planning anticipates future business and environmental demands on an organization and provides qualified people to fill needed positions.

Human resource planning is a process, not merely a component of a manager's job description. As a process, human resource planning focuses on identifying an organization's human resource needs under changing conditions and developing the interventions and initiatives necessary to satisfy those needs. This activity maintains organization continuity, vis-à-vis human resources, over an extended period of time, focusing on career pathing, succession planning, selecting the right person for the right job, and blending high-potential career actions. Human resource planning remains largely the exclusive domain of managers with limited solicited employee input. Those responsible for HR planning are strategists attempting to address the question, "What's best for the organization as a whole, both now and in the future?" Employees may serve as valuable resources during these activities if their input and insight are requested.

An organization's long-term success depends on its employees' competencies, which can either be developed internally or acquired on the open market. Planning for long-term use and development of human resources proves a complex activity that requires careful analysis and forecasting skill. To complicate the process, human resource planning pervades the entire organization because it requires input, involvement, and action by leaders, managers, and staff.

Human resource planning is a process of systematically organizing the future, of putting into place a plan designed to address upcoming performance problems or productivity and quality requirements. By addressing unknown variables, organizations align and structure their future to guarantee specific and certain outcomes. Failing to do so leads the organization along an uncertain path and jeopardizes the firm's future success. As the saying goes, if we fail to plan, we plan to fail.

Human resource planning is integrated with the organization's strategic plan and other organization-wide initiatives, revealing a strong interdependency among HR activities such as job analysis, recruitment, initial screening, interviewing process, selection, orientation, placement, the learning and change process, career development, compensation and rewards, and employee growth and development. The result? Improved employee self-esteem, career satisfaction, and motivation. The integrative approach enables human resource planning to positively impact the type and quality of people needed to ensure success.

Human Resource Planning Objective: To Hire, Select, and Promote Qualified Performers. Planning for long-term utilization and development of human resources requires careful analysis and forecasting expertise. Human resource planning entails anticipating future business conditions and having suf-ficient human resources to satisfy those needs. In essence, human resource planning attempts to ensure that organizations have the right people in the right place at the right time. By anticipating and addressing the unknown, organizations align and structure their futures to generate specific results in light of uncertainty. Failing to adequately plan for needed human resources, then, potentially jeopardizes a firm's future.

Too often, the hiring or promotion process reflects a popularity contest that ignores the critical skills necessary for success on the job. Successful organizations analyze job requirements and "hire the competencies" identified as success factors. Queries such as "Tell us your greatest strength," "Name your biggest weakness," or "Why do you want to work here?" won't reveal how an employee will deal with an irate customer or how a manager will handle conflict, motivate staff, or procure additional resources for the organization. Hiring according to competencies involves designing and asking questions that specifically uncover the skills (or lack thereof) identified in job analysis that an individual needs to be successful, long-term, in the position. For example, managers are often responsible for employees' motivation, development, and rewards. Appropriate queries that reveal skills in this area include the following:

- Specifically describe the techniques you have personally used to motivate employees, and then describe the results.
- Describe a situation in which you were able to motivate an employee at risk. Explain the specific techniques you used and the results you achieved.
- How do you personally get involved in or promote employee development?
- Describe the nonmonetary ways in which you reward employees for exemplary performance. Which rewards have been most effective and why?
- For what type of behaviors have your previously rewarded employees? Why do you feel that these behaviors were worthy of rewards?

Situation-specific, skill-based questions such as these allow interviewers to make informed hiring and promotion decisions focused on meeting organizational needs. It is important to note that "years of experience" doesn't necessarily mean that the candidate successfully met the requirements of the position. We have all worked for "experienced" managers who struggled in their positions, failed to achieve desired individual or organizational goals, and/or failed to develop positive working relationships with their colleagues, subordinates, or superiors. These individuals are often reassigned within their current organizations or promoted, or they seek and secure similar employment elsewhere—in spite of their deficiencies in performance. Poor recruiting and selection techniques lead to poor hiring and promotion decisions.

Components of Human Resource Planning. At the heart of human resource planning, recruiting, selection, and orientation is enhancing an organization's readiness and renewal capabilities, which are the precursors of success. Without human resource planning, an organization is steering blind, certain to run aground and seriously jeopardize its crew, cargo, and anything or anyone who has the misfortune of getting in its path.

Traditional organizations seldom cite organizational renewal or competitive readiness as reasons for conducting human resource planning. Some organizations do, however, mention these factors as reasons human resource planning is important. Most organizations believe in planning for future human resource needs and possibilities. They do so to improve business results and remain at full alert, poised to do battle at a moment's notice.

Human resource planning, recruiting, and selection determine the type, quantity, and quality of human resources needed to ensure organizational success. Thus, human resource professionals and organizational leaders engage in a series of related steps to guarantee that appropriate human resources are identified, recruited, selected, and developed to achieve performance success. The process begins with analysis of the factors that influence human resource planning, such as the business needs of the organization, competitive pressures, and future human resource requirements. Once these factors are identified, you analyze the conditions impacting current and future organizational success via internal and external environmental analysis—which reveals the organization's strengths, weaknesses, opportunities, and threats.

Next, a talent inventory reveals employees' skills, knowledge, abilities, and potential and how they are currently being used. Job analysis follows—which identifies the performance outputs, standards, and activities required of each job and the competencies needed by employees to successful execute them. These criteria serve as job-requirement data for which recruiting plans are designed, as measurement criteria useful in initial screening and interviewing of available candidates, and as the final determinant in selecting new employees. Another important criterion, personnel growth and developmental readiness, is a critical attitudinal element that must be identified during the screening, interviewing, and selection processes. Once selected, employees participate in orientation programs designed to socialize them within the organization and help them with placement on the job. Finally, organizations link the human resource planning process with the performance coaching and management process. In this way, each process impacts the others, providing continuous feedback that fosters organization renewal and enhances competitive readiness. Each step, its corresponding activities, and its outcomes are examined throughout this chapter.

Influences on Human Resource Planning. Several reasons exist for the increasing interest in human resource planning. They include

- shortage of the qualified, talented, experienced personnel needed to progress to senior management levels;
- the substantial cost of relocating personnel and the high cost of recruiting talented managers and leaders;
- the cost of implementing employee layoffs or reducing the labor force; and
- shortages of specialized technical personnel needed for growth and expansion.

Performance coaches are becoming more involved in the proper allocation and development of human resources.

Organizational Strategic Goals and Objectives

Jobs are designed to help organizations achieve their strategic business goals and objectives, which are the targets of the performance coaching and management process and measures of the entire organization's success. Positions that fail to fulfill a strategic need waste valuable resources while yielding little value. Job assignments, therefore, must be carefully analyzed to assure their contribution to organization success. In this way, employees are forever linked to the organization's strategy, guaranteeing direct, positive impact on organizational results.

Performance Goals and Objectives. The organization's strategic goals and objectives should drive creation of job-specific goals that help the organization achieve success. Each and every job within an organization should fulfill several key goals, regardless of who occupies the position.

A goal is a global statement of purpose and direction toward which all job tasks are directed. Goals define outcomes in terms of end products or results, act as continual points of reference, and keep all objectives and associated work on track. Work goals enable employees to stay focused on desired results, also promoting agreement and commitment with regard to performance outcomes. Performance goals represent the specific expectations of organizations, departments, and employees. Further, goal statements help you and your employees know that a successful outcome has been achieved. Performance goals, then, reveal what the end will look like.

Goal setting, although a valuable activity, is often improperly executed. Goals are incomplete without guidance for achievement, also called standards or expectations. Goals focus on measurable desired results and answer the question, "how much?" Common goals, for example, address acceptable revenues, profit levels, or the need to reduce the budget by a specific percent. Standards and expectations, on the other hand, reveal how and at what level of quality.

Employee-specific, or personal, goals address the knowledge, skill, education, talents, and ambitions of individuals on a personal level. Employees, for example, often include among their personal goals the desire to learn new software programs, write creatively or technically, or develop relationships with local businesses. As with most successful events, goal setting is a process. Effective goals are, however, S.M.A.R.T.—that is specific, measurable, action-oriented, realistic, and time-based. Job-related S.M.A.R.T. goals support the department or division's mission and goals, which in turn help the organization achieve its mission, goals, and objectives.

Material, Financial, and Human Resources

Employees rely on material, financial, and other human resources to complete tasks. Resources include information, equipment, computers, budgets, tools, and any other components necessary to perform the job. Employees working in outdated buildings or struggling organizations, for example, often complain of poor (or no) technology, lack of appropriate supplies, insufficient budgets, or no opportunities for professional development. Organizations that set high goals yet provide their employees with inadequate resources sabotage their efforts, which often leads to poor morale and performance. Thus, the performance coaching and management process is greatly improved by identifying the resources required to perform a specific job or set of jobs.

Material Resources. Material resources include the technology, information, tools, and equipment necessary for employees to perform their jobs. Material resources include anything critical to the generation of performance outputs (internal and external products or services) and can also include component parts and other vital elements of the production and service processes. Most critically, material resources must be available in the quantity and quality sufficient to produce outputs (products and services) at acceptable levels. We also include time and interaction exchanges between working parties in the equation because they are essential factors in the production and service processes, and finally, material resources must be available in a timely manner as to expedite the processes.

Financial Resources. One of the most important resources in the performance coaching and management process is financial, which determines the support available for each job classification within an organization. Adequate financial resources provide the freedom and flexibility needed when improving or reengineering performance processes and procedures. Typically, financial resources are linked to revenue growth and increased profitability. Financial resources primarily include cash and other remunerations used to underwrite the cost of production. Finally, they are directly related to the mission and strategy of an organization and to the execution of its business plan.

Human Resources. *Human resources* refers to the individuals employed by an organization. Unlike the typical straightforward, standard measures used to value fixed and liquid assets, organizations lack widely acceptable means by which to value employees and their contributions. For example, employees cannot be depreciated like physical resources and, more important, are seldom reflected in the net worth of an organization. However, employees are more important than material and financial resources, for their talent determines an organization's success. Unfortunately, some managers overlook this fact because employees are not used to reflect the organization's prosperity. Forward-thinking managers and organizations are aware that employees have value and consider employees in their asset portfolio. As a result, many recognize the importance of improving employees' knowledge, competencies, skills, and attitudes to improve the overall success of the firm.

As a performance coach, you have two critical responsibilities with respect to human resources. First, you assess employees' capacity, which includes their collective skills, knowledge, and abilities. This task requires identification of employees' current employment information, significant work experiences, specialized training, language skills, educational background (including degrees, licenses, and certifications), and growth and development plans (past and present). Identifying the capacity of employees enables you to distinguish employee proficiencies and establish a reliable baseline of human capital. Once this is determined, performance assignment decisions are made regarding the specific capacity of individual employees or the aggregate of employees' competencies. Accordingly, you can make decisions regarding future external recruiting efforts necessary to eliminate skill and knowledge gaps. Second, you enhance employees' capabilities, expanding their personal and professional potential, awareness, and insight. One of the best ways to facilitate individual capability is to create learning systems that focus on strengths while managing weaknesses,[2] a topic that is discussed in greater detail later in this chapter. Effective learning systems encourage employees to tackle challenging projects that increase their skill, which continues to develop their strengths via advanced training and new assignments. At the same time, partnering, preventing, and delegating strategies should be identified and incorporated to help employees manage their weaknesses.[3]

Performance Coaching

Performance coaching is a series of one-to-one exchanges between managers and their employees designed to solve problems, maximize opportunities, incorporate change, and improve performance. Performance coaching requires supervisors and managers to constantly shift among the roles of trainer, career advisor, strategist, and performance appraiser. Each role enhances employee self-esteem as it helps organizations achieve better results. During this phase of performance coaching and performance management, you accomplish the responsibilities and apply the competencies of each of the performance coaching roles.

Effective coaching is a continuous process, not an occasional conversation, that equips employees with the tools, knowledge, and opportunities they need to develop themselves and to be more productive employees. Performance coaches do so by working one-on-one with employees, guiding individuals to learn for themselves, and coordinating resources and learning activities through which employees are able to maximize their growth and development potential.

Performance Execution

The next step in the performance coaching and management process is to examine the performance execution of employees. This can be a straightforward and simple activity if the term *performance* is properly understood. *Perform* means "to begin and carry through to completion; to take action in accordance with the requirements of; fulfill. *Performance* means something performed; an accomplishment."[4] Thus, performance is synonymous with accomplishments, outcomes, or results. Performance is measured in terms of outcomes such as productivity or product costs.

Performance should not be confused with other concepts, such as work activities, behaviors, duties, competencies, or responsibilities. A work activity is a task or series of tasks taken to achieve results, and a behavior is an observable action. A duty is a moral obligation to perform, whereas a work activity has a definite beginning, middle, and end. A competency is an area of knowledge or skill that is critical for producing key performance outputs; responsibility is an action or a result for which one is accountable.

As previously discussed, every job consists of four elements: performance activities, outputs, standards, and competency maps. Once the elements are designed and aligned in proper order in the production or service delivery sequence, employees use their competencies to engage in performance activities for the purpose of generating performance outputs at an acceptable performance standard. Performance execution is, quite simply, the implementation of performance activities by employees at all levels in a firm.

Performance Appraisal

Performance coaches and employees should work closely together during a performance appraisal. This requires creating a partnership focused on identifying the strengths and weaknesses of the employee and the creation of an action plan that builds on strengths and manages weaknesses. A mutually beneficial partnership allows both parties to build a trusting, collaborative relationship that helps individuals identify performance-development opportunities. In this way, performance coaches solicit the involvement and support of employees in their growth and development. Moreover, performance coaches enjoy better outcomes when employees willingly participate in their own action planning.

Performance-appraisal interviews occasionally fail to yield positive outcomes because the interviewer focuses on personal characteristics and personalities rather than performance. Another reason for disappointing outcomes involves dwelling on employees' past actions instead of focusing on future performance. Although past performance *does* provide a means of sculpting and structuring the future, a coach's attention should be on future performance behaviors.

The following general guidelines can help performance coaches prepare for the actual interview process. These guidelines establish an environment exuding respect for individuals and their contributions during the term evaluated. They also serve as a reminder of the participatory emphasis of performance-appraisal interviews, reinforcing their developmental nature. To ensure successful evaluation interviews, performance coaches should establish and maintain rapport with their employees, explain clearly the purpose of the interview, and encourage employees to share their opinions and ideas so that their concerns are addressed (see Table 5.1). Next, they listen actively, without interruption, to employees' opinions and ideas, avoid confrontation or arguments that lead to negative or destructive discourse, and focus on performance, not personalities. They confront (not criticize or blame), focus on future (not past performance), and emphasize individual strengths as well as areas needing improvement. Finally, they terminate the interview on a positive note, when all parties reach agreement.

Five Stages of Performance Appraisals. The performance coach begins the performance-appraisal process by providing an overview of how the discussion will unfold, including steps to be followed during the meeting and the rules for engagement. Engagement rules include two-way

Table 5.1
Individuals' Concerns during a Performance Appraisal

The halo effect is the tendency to overrate a favored employees, which can occur for a variety of reasons:

- *Recency*—Allowing a recent positive event to distort judgment of the individual's entire performance.
- *Blind spot effect*—Overlooking performance deficiencies because the organization leader likes the employee for some reason.
- *Compatibility*—Overlooking negative performance because an individual is easy to work with, has a pleasing manner, or has a highly desired personality.
- *Previous outstanding performance*—Previous success overshadows current performance
- *Similar to me*—rating a person highly because of perceived similarities to oneself.
- *Favoritism*—Allowing poor performance to be overshadowed by qualities the organization leader personally finds appealing in the employee.
- *Overemphasis*—Giving too much weight to one outstanding factor, good or bad.
- *No-complaint bias*—An average individual has received no negative criticisms or complaints (e.g., no news is good news).
- *One-asset person*—Certain characteristics such as advanced degrees or impressive appearance may be ranked higher than work performance.
- *High-potential effect*—People who *could* achieve or accomplish a great deal are given undue consideration.
- *Leniency*—Some evaluators fail to adequately address poor performance by being too "forgiving."

communication, open and honest dialogue, candor, and substantive discussions based on actual performance supported by documentation. Once an overview has been provided, performance appraisals entail five steps:

Stage 1: The employee shares his or her perspective and assessment of past performance.
Stage 2: The performance coach shares his or her assessment and identifies strengths, weaknesses, and areas requiring improvement.
Stage 3: The performance coach and employee compare assessments, identifying similarities and differences.
Stage 4: The performance coach and employee develop an action plan (growth and development plan) for meeting goals, including changes in performance as well as growth and development planning activities.
Stage 5: The performance coach and employee establish progress-review schedule and activities.

Performance Appraisal Forms.   Gathering information and materials relevant to the discussion helps frame performance-appraisal interviews. Most organizations use simple appraisal or review forms that allow for numerical ranking of various characteristics or skills. Many of these forms impede the developmental nature desired of the performance-appraisal process. In fact, appraisal forms discourage the free exchange of ideas and violate the spirit of performance appraisals.

These forms come in every shape and size and typically have one common characteristic—the desire to make the review process as simple as possible. Organizations have attempted to make the performance-appraisal process a painless activity—encouraging performance coaches to assign a "number" for employees in every possible category. These "easy" or "painless" attempts at performance appraisal simply compound the difficulty many managers have with confronting poor performance. Numbers don't explain the problem, nor do they suggest solutions.

Simple numerical forms are far more damaging than beneficial. It makes more sense for an organization leader to start with a blank sheet of paper (with identified performance goals and standards for all important categories) and pen a performance appraisal (see the developmental appraisal form in Figure 5.2) than to waste time filling out a performance appraisal form that has little or no value as a developmental tool. Few if any performance problems have been resolved through the use of such forms, which serve only as a mechanism by which to defend organizations during litigation. Because these are not developmental tools, they should not be the sole basis of performance appraisals.

Employee _____   For the Period _____ to _____

Supervisor _____

Employee goals for the past period:

1.

2.

3.

Accomplishments (goals, other achievements):

1.

2.

3.

4.

Shortfalls (goals, others):

1.

2.

Employee Signature _____   Date _____

Supervisor Signature _____   Date _____

Figure 5.2 Developmental Appraisal Form

If performance coaches lack the time, energy, or dedication necessary to use the appraisal process in a constructive, developmental manner, it ceases to be of value. However, we understand organizations' needs to defend themselves from individuals who feel as though they have been improperly treated. Consequently, it makes more sense to have comprehensive documentation of an individual's performance and the coach's attempt to correct that performance than to use a simple 1–5 evaluation form. It is more important to have documented work samples and observable evaluation data than a simple, possibly biased, definitely one-sided scale appraisal form. When appraisals are done in a constructive, helpful manner, most if not all employees will improve their performance.

Certainly, there are occasions when an employee has been improperly selected for a job or his or her skills and knowledge have been mismatched to job activities or performance outputs required. This has little or nothing to do with performance appraisals, but rather is a recruiting and selection dilemma that may need to be addressed within the firm. We strongly urge organizations to eliminate the use of forms that provide weak support of their legal position. Instead, turn performance appraisals into a tool to enhance employee growth and development.

360-Degree Feedback. One type of appraisal gaining popularity is 360-degree feedback, also called multisource or multi-rater feedback (see Figure 5.3). This kind of feedback is a critical component of an in-depth performance appraisal or review process. Multi-rater feedback taps the collective wisdom of those who work most closely with the employee: supervisor, peers, subordinates, and customers (internal and external). These individuals provide feedback on critical competencies, specific behaviors, and skills, which gives the employee a clear understanding of personal strengths and areas needing development.

Proponents of multi-rater feedback claim that it provides a more accurate assessment of an employee's performance—and by those who interact with the employee in a variety of work-related circumstances. Input by colleagues and customers is more reliable, valid, and credible than that of a manager with whom the employee interacts infrequently.

360-degree feedback addresses performance (how am I doing?) and performance management (what are my areas of strength and those needing improvement?). It provides a clear picture of critical skills or competencies, unlike single raters (supervisors), who tend to generalize or group large amounts of specific information together. Because the feedback is so specific, employees can track their progress on each competency.

Biases of Performance Evaluators. Performance appraisals are only as good as the evaluator. Therefore, it is important to consider the possible biases performance coaches bring to the evaluation process. Although these can be positive or negative in nature, they nevertheless produce a distorted, erroneous view of the employee, the employee's performance, and the employee's career opportunities. Biases may affect any or all performance appraisals and must be guarded against at all times to

Designing a 360-Degree Feedback Program

    I.   Assess satisfaction with and usefulness of current process
    II.   Appoint design team
    III.   Develop a competency-based survey instrument
    IV.   Train participants in how to provide feedback to and receive feedback from others
    V.   Conduct evaluations
    VI.   Score evaluations and create reports
    VII.   Conduct user assessment or evaluation of 360-degree effectiveness
    VIII.   Refine, refine, refine

Evaluation of the Current Review or Appraisal Process

N=don't know **1**=strongly disagree **2**=disagree **3**=agree **4**=strongly agree

1. The current performance feedback and measurement process provides me with information that . . .

a. is useful for development.	N	1	2	3	4
b. is useful for review or appraisal.	N	1	2	3	4
c. motivates me.	N	1	2	3	4
d. is valuable for me.	N	1	2	3	4
e. is fair to me.	N	1	2	3	4
f. is fair to others.	N	1	2	3	4
g. is a complete assessment.	N	1	2	3	4
h. is an accurate assessment.	N	1	2	3	4
i. provides safeguards for fairness.	N	1	2	3	4

2. Overall, I am satisfied with   N   1   2   3   4
the current process.

3. Comments:

About you (optional):

Time in job: ___under 1 year ___1–3 years___4–5 years
    ___6–10 years   ___11+ years

Figure 5.3 Example of the 360-Degree Feedback Assessment Process and Form

Time in firm: ___under 1 year ___1–5 years___6–10 years
                        ___11–20 years ___21+ years

Gender: ___male   ___female

Appoint design team

Members of the design team should

- represent all organizational levels (management, employees, and so on),
- include at least one well-known skeptic,
- possess strong communications and language skills, and
- be high performers.

The team's job is to answer the following question: What are the critical competencies our organization will need in the future to sustain our competitive advantage in the marketplace?

Develop a competency-based feedback instrument

The team defines the individual behaviors that support broad organization goals and objectives. Because competencies often need some definition, the team then develops statements associated with each value, which become questions on the survey. These statements should be clearly written, brief, and should cover *observable* behaviors.

Agenda for feedback-instrument design team

Activity 1—Develop competencies
List critical behavioral criteria. For example, what behaviors are critical to achieving the organization's mission this year and beyond? List core and supporting competencies.

Activity 2—Combine similar constructs
Sort behaviors into clusters or groups.

Activity 3—Refine
Reconsider groupings and items within groups.

Activity 4—Work on behavioral descriptors
Develop behavioral descriptions for the behaviors.

Activity 5—Place final touches on survey instrument
Design cover page, instructions, and so on, along with performing alpha testing. Make sure to do the following:

- Match competencies to the organization's vision and values.
- Use the organization's common language; keep it simple so that all understand.

(Continued)

- Group similar content together, such as competencies associated with team-work.
- Keep the competency set simple and short.
- Use only those competencies necessary for employee success in a particular job.

Employee _____   **Date** _____

Supervisor _____

Indicate your relationship to the individual you are rating:

☐ self
☐ manager
☐ colleague/peer
☐ direct report (I am evaluating my manager)
☐ internal customer (I am evaluating a colleague outside of my department)
☐ external customer
☐ other

You have been identified by the person being rated in this evaluation as someone who can provide valuable input to the employee on his or her performance. Your responses will remain anonymous; only composite information will be provided to the employee. Please return this form to ____(supervisor)_____ ___ by ____(date)_____.

How well does this person perform the competencies described in the following sections? Please use the following scale for your evaluation. "N" is appropriate when you are unfamiliar with behavior in certain areas.

(5) **Exceptional**—This individual consistently exceeds behavior and skills expectations in this area.

(4) **High**—This individual meets most and exceeds some of the behavior and skills expectations in this area.

(3) **Meets**—This individual meets a majority of the behavior and skills expectations in this area for this job. There is generally a positive perspective toward responsibilities.

(2) **Low**—This individual meets some behavior and skills expectations in this area but sometimes falls short.

(1) **Poor**—This individual consistently fails to reach behavior and skills expectations in this area.

(N) **"Not applicable"** or **"Not observed"**

CUSTOMER SERVICE

Treats customers like business partners	N	1	2	3	4	5
Presents ideas simply and clearly	N	1	2	3	4	5
Listens actively to internal and external customers	N	1	2	3	4	5
Solicits and provides constructive and honest feedback	N	1	2	3	4	5
Keeps others informed	N	1	2	3	4	5
Balances requests with business requirements	N	1	2	3	4	5
Responds to appropriate needs of customers	N	1	2	3	4	5

Comments: _____
_____
_____

TEAMWORK

Supports team goals	N	1	2	3	4	5
Puts interest of team ahead of self	N	1	2	3	4	5
Builds consensus and shares relevant information	N	1	2	3	4	5
Builds and maintains productive working relationships	N	1	2	3	4	5
Treats others fairly	N	1	2	3	4	5
Actively seeks involvement from and uses input from people with different perspectives	N	1	2	3	4	5
Recognizes and respects the contributions and needs of each individual	N	1	2	3	4	5

Comments: _____
_____
_____

BUSINESS AND INDIVIDUAL SKILLS

Demonstrates broad business knowledge and skills	N	1	2	3	4	5
Acts to add value to the business	N	1	2	3	4	5
Recognizes problems and identifies underlying causes	N	1	2	3	4	5

(Continued)

Makes timely decisions	N	1	2	3	4	5
Coaches and develops others	N	1	2	3	4	5
Is trustworthy, open, and honest	N	1	2	3	4	5
Visualizes the present and future and develops strategies to get there	N	1	2	3	4	5

Comments: _____
_____
_____

PROFESSIONAL AND TECHNICAL KNOWLEDGE

Demonstrates professional and technical expertise	N	1	2	3	4	5
Shares expertise with others	N	1	2	3	4	5
Organizes work	N	1	2	3	4	5
Acts dependably to get things done right the first time	N	1	2	3	4	5
Improves existing processes or introduces new methods	N	1	2	3	4	5
Actively increases personal skills, knowledge, and technical base	N	1	2	3	4	5
Motivates others to achieve results through example and encouragement	N	1	2	3	4	5

Comments: _____
_____
_____

RESOURCE MANAGEMENT

Takes initiative to make things happen	N	1	2	3	4	5
Takes informed, calculated risks	N	1	2	3	4	5
Makes well-reasoned, timely decisions	N	1	2	3	4	5
Follows through to deliver results	N	1	2	3	4	5
Uses resources efficiently	N	1	2	3	4	5

Communicates a clear direction   N 1 2 3 4 5

Anticipates and prepares for change   N 1 2 3 4 5

Comments: _____

_____

_____

Overall comments regarding this individual and his or her performance and
behavior: _____

_____

_____

_____

prevent unsubstantiated, poorly representative assessments. See Tables
5.2 and 5.3 for a list of biases common during performance appraisals.

Effective performance coaches recognize potential biases and pitfalls
and try to eliminate them from performance judgments. This can best be
accomplished by establishing specific, concise performance standards that
are attached to performance outputs and activities. Performance standards
provide employees with the type of information necessary for them to
make performance judgments and determine whether they are producing
the kinds of results the organization desires. Performance coaches benefit
because performance standards provide the criteria necessary to conduct
bias-free evaluations.

Several other pitfalls and biases also exist, including stereotyping, subjective performance standards, and opportunity biases. Stereotyping involves basing performance appraisals on fixed perceptions of performance
rather than on actual achievements. Subjective performance standards
allow performance coaches and employees to hold different perceptions
of performance outputs and success. Finally, opportunity bias occurs when
performance coaches do not have adequate time to judge an employee's performance firsthand. Therefore, judgments are based on assumptions, central
tendencies of a work group, or singular performance outputs or activities.

Growth and Development Plans

The fundamental purpose of a performance appraisal is to identify
ways to improve the employee's performance. A growth and development action plan allows employees to maximize their strengths, minimize
weaknesses, and overcome deficiencies, which is the focus of step 4 in the
performance-appraisal process (see Figure 5.4).

Table 5.2
Halo Effect

The horn effect is the opposite of the halo effect—the tendency to rate a person lower than circumstances justify. Some specific examples include the following:

- *Recency*—Allowing a recent negative event or poor performance to distort judgment of a person's entire work.
- *Grouping* (tarnishing or whitewashing)—Painting all employees in a work group with the same perceptional brush.
- *Prejudice*—Allowing good performance to be overshadowed by an individual's traits or qualities that the organization leader finds unattractive.
- *Guilt by association*—Employees are prejudged because of the company they keep.
- *Dramatic incident effect*—One recent mistake or poor performance offsets the entire year's achievements.
- *Difficult employee effect*—Irritating, contrary, or opposite personality characteristics overshadow actual performance.
- *Maverick effect*—The nonconformist may be downgraded because he or she is different.
- *Weak team effect*—Exemplary performance may be downplayed because the individual belongs to an underachieving work group.
- *Unrealistic expectations effect*—Expectations that are too high are brought about by the evaluator's perfectionism.
- *Personality trait effect*—Individuals exhibit certain personality traits considered inappropriate.
- *Self-comparison effect*—Bias resulting from differentiation in the way the supervisor perceives a job should be carried out.

In many respects, an action plan is simply the process of establishing the parameters, conditions, and specifications required to improve performance. Questions to consider include the following:

- What are the stated and understood performance goals for the future?
- What steps can the employee take to build on identified strengths?
- What specific steps must be taken to improve performance?
- How much improvement is needed, and by when?
- How can performance coaches assist employees in creation of formal action plans?
- What resources (time, money, training, and so on) are necessary to execute the action plan, and who is responsible for providing them?
- What support is required of organization administrators, leaders, and managers?

Table 5.3
Horn Effect

Before conducting a performance appraisal, you should carefully consider seven questions employees are challenged to answer. These questions focus performance appraisals, preventing verbal "free for alls" common during unplanned meetings. These seven represent the most prevalent employee concerns and are likely to surface during the performance appraisal:

1. How am I doing?
2. What can I do to improve?
3. Do I have a chance for advancement?
4. What will be expected of me prior to my next performance appraisal?
5. How can my work be evaluated during this time?
6. What kind of help or attention can I expect from my performance coaches or supervisor?
7. What changes are likely to occur within the organization that will affect my job or performance in the months ahead, and how will they affect me?

The reviewer should carefully consider each of these questions prior to entering into the review process.

The best action plans are developed by the employees. Individuals are more likely to support the decisions or initiatives in which they have had input.

The success of an action plan depends on five requirements. First, employees must *want* to change their performance behavior. That is, they must have the desire to acquire new knowledge and skills or build upon existing ones.

Second, action plans must

- identify employees' performance improvement needs,
- determine the barriers that prevent learning acquisition and transfer,
- address cultural issues that reduce employee motivation,
- identify conflicting job tasks and activities that diminish learning, and
- provide performance feedback and reinforcement on the job.

These activities are primarily the responsibility of performance coaches, who are challenged to create cooperative learning environments that are conducive to employee growth and development. Such environments amplify learning opportunities by providing employees with a secure, comfortable atmosphere that encourages and holds them accountable for acquiring and applying new knowledge and skills.

Employee _____   For the Period _____ to _____
Supervisor _____

Employee goals for the upcoming period:

1.

2.

3.

Employee actions / Date: **Supervisor actions / Support / Date:**

1.

2.

3

Employee Signature _____   Date _____
Supervisor Signature _____   Date _____

Figure 5.4 Performance Growth and Development Action Plan

Third, employees share in action planning by realizing that they are ultimately responsible for acquiring learning and transferring it to the job. Employees must identify the knowledge and skills they desire to change and must have the desire and ability to manage their own learning and work environments. This type of self-discipline is not present in all individuals, which is one of the reasons learning transfer does not occur in every situation. The success of action planning depends on the employees' aptitude for acquiring new knowledge and skills and their self-control and discipline, high achievement needs, and motivation to use new skills on the job.

Fourth, encouragement and reinforcement from performance coaches is needed in order for employees to improve their performance. Occasionally, individuals are afraid to participate in developmental activities because they fear failure. Some employees lack the confidence to participate without encouragement or assistance, whereas others possess every intention of participating, but either are too disorganized or fall victim to procrastination. Manager or coach support often determines the success or failure rate of performance improvement.

Fifth, many employees fail to participate in action plans because they are not rewarded for their efforts. Although this is seemingly shortsighted, many are convinced that unless the firm is willing to recognize their efforts, changing their performance behaviors is unnecessary.

Most employees are willing to participate in organized action plans when all of these five requirements for behavioral change are satisfied. Performance coaches should make certain that employees know exactly what behavioral changes are expected, which skills need improvement, and what level of performance is required. Performance coaches must also make certain that learning acquisition can occur on or through the job and that employees will be given adequate support and encouragement as they struggle to integrate new knowledge and skills.

Compensation and Rewards

A compensation and reward philosophy should be based on rewarding employees for the "right" performance. In this way, organizations demonstrate their understanding that "the things that get rewarded get done."[5] This approach ensures that the organization will secure its desired outcomes. On the other hand, failure to reward the right behaviors leads to unsatisfactory outcomes.

A compensation and reward philosophy should be flexible enough to take into account the dynamic nature of the organization and other important system-wide activities. When this occurs, the compensation and reward program remains fluid and subject to review, alteration, or redesign. This approach encourages continuous compensation improvement that reflects the organization's culture, values, guiding principles, and strategic business goals and objectives. An effective compensation and reward philosophy defines *who* participates in compensation and reward decisions, whether decision making should be centralized with administrators or decentralized within departments, and whether performance coaches should be held accountable for their respective decisions and contributions to the compensation and reward program.

An effective compensation and reward philosophy takes into account each step of the organization's performance-management process. In this way, a compensation and reward approach allows organizations to (1) identify employees' needs and expectations, (2) design jobs that produce maximum results at the highest possible level of quality, (3) encourage performance coaches to build synergistic relationships with employees, (4) require performance coaches to conduct formal performance appraisals with employees, and (5) collaboratively create performance growth and development plans designed to enhance performance.

Developmental Compensation Philosophy—Rewarding Growth and Development. Compensation is designed to motivate employees to improve quality, responsiveness, and efficiency. This is certainly not a new concept. Developmental compensation has different aims—to promote individual employee growth and performance by

- being an extension of the organization's developmental philosophy;
- rewarding the "right things";
- linking compensation with organizational goals and objectives;
- creatively applying existing compensation methods, such as individual incentives or bonuses in new ways;
- being flexible and open to trying new compensation methods for existing or novel situations; and
- constantly monitoring and assessing its effectiveness and alignment with strategic business goals and objectives.

We strongly believe that employees are the organization's greatest assets. Consequently, organizations must develop long-term compensation and reward strategies that encourage employees to participate in performance growth and development activities that, in turn, encourage continuous learning and skill acquisition. Historically, compensation and reward programs have been performance-based, with little consideration given to rewarding individuals for continually enhancing their skills or competencies. However, compensation and reward programs can become a vehicle for increasing employee development as opposed to mere performance achievement. Of course, the intent is not to mitigate the importance of performance, but to clarify that performance without growth and development will stagnate or even decline. Shifting compensation and reward programs to encourage employee growth and development ensures that individuals' skills and competencies continue to evolve.

The shift from rewarding performance to rewarding growth and development involves a remarkable transformation. Successful evolution includes rewarding employees for applying what they have learned on the job *and* rewarding performance coaches who create environments conducive to learning transfer. By rewarding performance growth and development, organizations create environments that enhance continuous improvement and quality. This also enhances an organization's readiness to reinforce and encourage individuals who show the initiative to achieve performance results. When growth and development are encouraged, performance successes become an operational reality rather than a mere slogan.

Every organization takes a journey through the organizational life cycle, which is characterized by periods of birth, growth and expansion, maturity and stagnation, and decline. During eras of growth and expansion, organizational members reap a bountiful financial harvest. As a result, firms focus their attention on short-term performance results without considering the skills and competencies required to remain competitive over time. This emphasis harms the organization's effectiveness because it requires organization members to make decisions that encourage short-term gain at the expense of long-term strategic organizational health. Organizations that fail to perpetuate the growth phase experience stagnation and eventual decline. Thus, performance without growth and development prevents an organization from maintaining the growth phase.

Gilley et al.[6] provide a step-by-step framework for linking compensation and rewards to individual performance growth and development goals. The framework requires organizations to make certain that they have a clearly identified and defensible reward strategy for achieving desired results.

First, performance coaches need to work collaboratively with their employees to identify performance growth and development goals. It is important that these enable individuals to contribute to one or more of the organization's strategic goals and objectives. In this way, a clear linkage is established between growth and development plans and the achievement of organizational results. Performance growth and development then becomes an enhancement activity that promotes the firm's continued success.

Next, performance coaches determine whether proposed performance growth and development goals match the organization's compensation and reward strategy. If these two elements are incompatible, adjustments must be made in the organization's reward strategy, the employees' performance growth and development goals, or both. This step determines whether the organization's long-term reward strategy is congruent with employee development activities.

Third, performance coaches make certain that performance growth and development goals are specific, measurable, agreed upon, realistic, and time bound (S.M.A.R.T.). If for some reason these goals fail to meet such criteria, they should be reevaluated, clarified, and rewritten to ensure clarity and specificity.

Fourth, rewards must be substantial enough to motivate employees to continue professional development activities. Therefore, performance coaches must ascertain whether rewards indeed motivate employees to participate in performance growth and development activities. Those that fail to motivate individual participation in professional development activities should be redesigned, which can be accomplished through a variety of evaluation techniques, including focus groups, personal interviews, questionnaires, or small-group discussions.

Employees need positive feedback and reinforcement to guarantee their motivation to acquire new skills and competencies and transfer them to the job.[7] Positive feedback and reinforcement powerfully encourage employee participation and involvement. Absent feedback, employees make uninformed decisions regarding their performance, resulting in mistakes that can lead to disastrous results. Without feedback, employees do not know where they are, how they are doing, or whether they are applying new skills and knowledge appropriately. Feedback informs employees as to whether they are producing results on time, at the correct level of quality, and in the correct form.

Outcomes of the Performance Coaching and Management Process

Properly designed performance coaching and management processes build commitment and improve employee loyalty, gauge employee performance in relationship to performance standards or expectations, and directly link compensation and rewards to actual performance. The ultimate outcome of the performance coaching and management process is motivated and satisfied employees committed to achieving the organization's strategic goals and objective (see the last two boxes in Figure 5.1). Organizational results include increased revenue, improved quality, greater market share, or increased profitability. Simply, performance coaching helps employees resolve problems, improve performance, and most importantly, achieve their desired results, which enhances their self-esteem.

Enhancing Employee Self-Esteem

Perhaps one of the major obstacles in addressing the performance challenge is identifying ways of enhancing employees' self-esteem. The only way to truly integrate the components of the performance coaching and management process is to discover and implement means by which to grow and develop employees.

Four primary sources contribute to enhancing an employee's self-esteem:[8]

- Achievement, accomplishment, and mastery—Employees need opportunities to achieve or accomplish something meaningful. This may include acquiring new skills or knowledge, participating in creative endeavors, being granted new and exciting responsibilities, participating in visible, important projects, or providing their opinions and insights regarding the organization's direction.
- Power, control, and influence—Providing employees with opportunities to have influence over decisions, authority over others, and power and control greatly enhances their self-esteem. Many employees identify with the traditional symbols of success such as job titles, increased office space, and access to key decision makers.
- Being cared about and valued—Many employees go to work every day, hoping they will receive some type of positive affirmation for their existence. "Thank you" goes a long way. Unfortunately, some managers discount the importance of a positive relationship, regarding it as unnecessary or insignificant. For many employees, personal involvement is an essential source of self-esteem, and should be treated accordingly.
- Acting on values and beliefs—At the heart of every employee's behavior is a set of values and beliefs that guide their actions. These values and beliefs serve as a source of positive self-esteem for employees who are able to act consistently on them.

Each of these sources channels an employee's experiences to his or her overall self-esteem level. These four sources of self-esteem enable positive experiences to flow into a self-concept bucket. The more positive experiences employees have, the higher their self-esteem level will become. Eventually, employees' experiences either add to or subtract from their self-concept buckets, which either raises or lowers their level of self-esteem.

Negative experiences reduce employee self-esteem—the net effect is a lower self-concept, producing negative employees and poor outcomes. Employees cannot engage in positive interactions if they can't rebuild their self-esteem. If this cycle is allowed to continue, the result is angry, resentful employees who are fearful of management and the organization. These employees avoid taking risks, making recommendations for improvement, or engaging in professional growth and development opportunities. Consequently, performance coaches must find ways to fill their employees' self-concept buckets, enhance their career satisfaction, and motivate exceptional performance. The aforementioned four sources of self-esteem provide a solid basis for working effectively with employees.

CONCLUSION

In this chapter we examined the principles of performance improvement, which include performance–reward disconnect, performance confusion, and inspection failure, the benefits of performance management, and the performance coaching and management process. The performance coaching and management process consists of 10 integrative steps resulting in improved employee self-esteem, which enhances career satisfaction and motivation.

SIX

Practices in the Performance Coaching and Management Process

One of the most heated debates regarding the performance coaching and management process is whether it is a contingent or normative process. The contingent camp argues that performance coaches should allow employees to determine the direction of performance improvement, and performance coaches help employees achieve this end. In contrast, the significantly larger normative camp argues that, although the performance coaching and management process should be facilitative, performance coaches have a responsibility to recommend specific directions for performance improvement. They contend that the coaching and management process encourages the development of personal skills and competencies that the organization can utilize in its effort to remain competitive and productive. Accordingly, the ultimate benefit of the process is that it allows employees to become mature, psychologically healthy, and committed to the organization. Thus, the principal outcome of the performance coaching and management process is its development of people as well as organizations.

The normative approach represents a gentle shift toward a more humanistic treatment of all employees in that the direction of performance improvement is toward an organizational culture in which growth and development of employees is just as important as making a profit or staying within budget. In this culture, equal opportunity and fairness for people in the organization are commonplace. In fact, it is the rule rather than the exception. Such a culture associates authority more with knowledge and competence than with role or status while encouraging managers to exercise more participative than directive authority.

A normative approach to the performance coaching and management process creates an organizational culture in which employees are kept informed or at least have access to information, especially concerning matters that directly affect their jobs or them personally. Cooperative behavior is rewarded more frequently than competitive behavior. Performance improvement develops an organizational culture in which conflict is dealt with openly and systematically, rather than ignored, avoided, or handled in a typical win–lose fashion, while employees feel a sense of ownership of the organization's mission and objectives. A normative approach creates an environment in which employees are given as much autonomy and freedom to do their respective jobs as possible, to ensure both a high degree of individual motivation and accomplishment of organizational objectives. Finally, rewards are based on a system of both equality-fairness and equity-merit.

CRITICAL APPLICATIONS OF THE PERFORMANCE COACHING AND MANAGEMENT PROCESS

In chapters 1 through 5, we discussed several components of the performance coaching and management process, including enhancing performance, improving career development, career planning, enhancing employee self-esteem, facilitating and managing change, analyzing performance, improving performance appraisals, and creating growth and development plans. Next, we discuss specific applications of the performance coaching and management process.

Critical applications of the coaching and management process include creating performance teams, dealing with disagreements, overcoming excuses and performance barriers, improving delegation, implementing and managing learning, improving goal setting and decision making, and facilitating collaborative problem solving.

Creating Performance Teams

The performance coaching and management process enables coaches to create conditions in which work groups become performance teams.

A performance team is a small number of people with complementary skills who are committed to a common purpose, performance goals, and approaches for which they hold themselves mutually accountable. These elements define the size, membership requirements, outcomes, strategies, and evaluation process of performance teams. Performance teams increase the performance capacity of organizations by focusing on projects and business results, whereas work groups focus solely on task completion. Performance teams are assembled to produce results or a positive "win–loss record" for the organization. Wins come in many forms, such as increased market share, improved quality, better on-time delivery, and enhanced customer service. Performance teams discover creative ways of improving productivity, which in turn provides employees with growth and development opportunities. This difference is paramount in creating a developmental philosophy within the firm. Moreover, performance teams provide members with opportunities to build on their strengths through delegating and partnering activities. These principally separate performance teams from work groups.

Because performance teams are assembled to achieve specific, well-defined objectives (business results) they must have clearly defined roles and identified activities to follow. Every team member depends on his or her colleagues to perform their jobs to exact performance standards and on time. Therefore, performance teams are characterized by clarity.

Performance teams resolve job-related problems. As a result, these teams are responsible for exploring possibilities and alternatives, which requires a tremendous amount of autonomy and freedom to function successfully. Each team member must believe that his or her colleagues are being truthful and demonstrating a high degree of integrity during interactions. Team members must value and respect each other for their ideas, commitment, and contributions to guarantee the success of teams. These elements become the distinguishing characteristics, which

- allows team members to remain problem-focused,
- promotes more effective communications and coordination,
- improves the quality of collaborative outcomes, and
- leads to compensating work styles in which one team member picks up the slack that occurs when another member falters.

Performance teams are based on the belief that the people who do a job understand it well and are best equipped to improve the quality of their work. Performance teams allow employees to resolve many of the problems that negatively impact day-to-day operations. As such, the teams become a participatory management resource designed to systematically harness the brainpower of employees to solve organizational problems of productivity and quality. Performance teams are behaviorally based and represent performance coaches' awareness that employees can positively contribute to an organization. They demonstrate the importance of human resources by inviting participation.

Performance teams are results-oriented but are equally concerned about the development of people. This people-building philosophy is demonstrated through a sincere effort to provide employees with challenging problems to solve.

Once a performance team's purpose has been determined, it is important to design teams so that they can function effectively. Highly productive teams exhibit four distinctive features: (1) clear roles, responsibilities, and accountabilities; (2) an effective communication system that ensures easy access to information; (3) credible and documentable; and (4) methods for monitoring individual performance and providing feedback with an emphasis on fact-based judgments. Depending on the emphasis and purpose of a performance team, these features may vary.

The four cardinal principles of performance teams are as follows:

1. Performance teams have the autonomy and freedom to decide which problems they will address, allowing members the opportunity to support what they create.
2. Performance teams bring decision making closer to those who actually do the job, thereby allowing members to communicate to management what they feel are the solutions to problems facing the organization.
3. Performance teams encourage collective, collaborative problem solving, in which team members strive to create win–win solutions to difficult organizational problems.
4. Performance teams create working relationships based on trust.

Performance teams provide growth and development opportunities that create a synergistic partnership between employees and the organization. Accordingly, growth and development opportunities help employees improve their performance and productivity while helping the organization improve its productivity, quality, and profitability. As these occur, the firm has more financial resources to invest in its people, and the cycle of continuous growth and development continues.

Dealing with Disagreements, Excuses, and Performance Barriers

Performance appraisals and other the performance coaching and management process activities are designed to enhance performance, not place blame or accuse individuals of wrongful acts. Occasionally, disagreements become difficult to manage. At times, employees offer excuses for poor performance, fail to participate during the performance-appraisal interviews, want unavailable or unjustified promotions, desire groundless merit increases, feel that a performance problem is not important, or want to discuss irrelevant issues. When such difficulties surface, it is important to have a strategy for overcoming them. In the following sections, we examine each difficult situation separately and provide recommendations for dealing with employees in each circumstance.

Disagreement on the Performance-Appraisal Assessment. In this situation, both parties appear to be at an impasse. Performance coaches should initiate the following steps to reach agreement:

- Demonstrate understanding of the employee's point of view.
- Be flexible (willing to change your mind).
- Provide evidence to support your position or point of view, and allow the employee to provide evidence to support his or her position.
- Check for agreement.
- Allow the individual the opportunity to reverse his or her position without losing face.

If the employee continues to disagree, you should request that the employee express the disagreement in writing and provide suggestions for correcting the performance problem.

Excuses for Poor Performance. Sometimes we yield to the temptation to make excuses. They're quick and easy, and they absolve us of responsibility for our own poor performance. Coaches should (1) demonstrate understanding, (2) reach agreement with the employee that results are not satisfactory, (3) discuss with the employee what can be done about the problems, and (4) ask the employee for solutions to correct the performance problem.

Superficial Barriers to Improving Performance. Several superficial barriers impede performance. Let us examine a few of the most common ones.
    Believing the performance problem is not important—When an employee does not consider his or her performance a problem, consider the following to counteract this situation. First, demonstrate understanding of the employee's point of view. Second, confirm agreement on what has happened and discuss the impacts (on other employees and the organization)

of the performance problem. Third, check for agreement and ask for suggestions for correcting the performance problem.

Discussing irrelevant issues—Overcoming this situation requires you to recommend another, more appropriate time to discuss irrelevant issues while demonstrating understanding of the employee's needs. Performance coaches need to redirect the employee on the subject by asking focused questions pertaining to his or her exact performance.

Failing to participate during the performance-appraisal interview—Lack of employee participation may be promulgated by a variety of factors, from shyness to stress to intimidation, and so on. When this occurs, reestablish rapport, ask open-ended questions, pause, and absorb responses. Rephrase employee responses, ask for agreement, minimize criticism or disagreements, stress the importance of the employee's perspective, indicate the value of his or her perspective, and encourage the employee's full participation and cooperation.

Demanding unavailable or unjustified promotions—Performance coaches should support the employee's enthusiasm, clarify organizational realities, and discuss requirements for promotion (e.g., knowledge, skills, advanced degree, expertise, and so on). Finally, help employees formulate a plan to meet requirements and advise that there are no guarantees that a promotion is imminent.

Wanting to Discuss Unjustified Merit Increases

Many employees erroneously believe that their (poor) performance justifies an increase in compensation and that they have performed at an acceptable or exemplary level. Others feel deserving of merit increases simply because of tenure. Under these circumstances, discuss pay-for-performance plans or compensation policies that exist within the organization. Compare an employee's actual performance with performance standards established for the job. Further, clarify the organization's position and ability regarding merit increases, addressing whether the employee has met or exceeded the standards necessary to receive such an increase.

Improving Delegation

Delegation can be defined as appointing someone to operate on your behalf. Delegation is a primary responsibility of managers who are familiar with the organization and who have the authority to make things happen. Achieving this end requires performance coaches to delegate duties, tasks, and responsibilities to their employees. Delegation requires that a performance coach have trust in his or her employees, confidence in their abilities, and an understanding of performance improvement's impact on an organization, which can only be gained through firsthand exposure acquired by performance coaches via years of experience.

Delegation is simply assigning an employee a task or responsibility that is otherwise part of someone else's job. Consequently, when performance coaches delegate a work assignment to a employee, they remain accountable for the outcome. That is, tasks and responsibilities may be delegated, but accountability cannot be. Accountability rests with the individual who was originally assigned the task or responsibility—typically the manager, or coach. Therefore, it is important to have an open, honest discussion about the accountability relationship that occurs as a result of the delegation. In this way, an employee knows exactly what he or she is accountable for, and to whom.

Following these steps improves delegation activities:

1. Decide what to delegate—Choose a job or task that is realistic yet challenging.
2. Plan the delegation—Review all essential details and decisions, determine appropriate feedback controls, provide for training and coaching, and establish performance standards.
3. Select the right person—Consider the employee's interests, skills, abilities, and qualifications to complete the assignment and consider what support or training is needed.
4. Delegate effectively—Clarify the results expected and priorities involved; specify level of authority granted; and identify the importance of the assignment, of feedback, and of reporting requirements.
5. Follow up—Insist on results but not perfection, demand timely performance reports, encourage independence, don't short-circuit or take back the assignment, and reward good performance.

The first step in the delegation cycle involves identifying tasks and responsibilities to be delegated. This often requires performance coaches to analyze jobs, determine which tasks are most appropriate for delegation, and clarify the expected results. Once these steps are completed, coaches should meet with their employees to explain their work-assignment rationale and allow the employees to ask questions or share opinions.

Second, outline the level of authority being granted to your employees. This answers the question, "What authority can the employee exercise to accomplish the task at hand?" The authority granted in a delegation depends on the employee's experience and the performance coach's confidence in his or her skills and abilities. Confidence refers to the extent to which you trusts the employee's abilities based on his or her performance history. The combination of confidence and experience determines the level of authority to grant.

A model illustrating this relationship places confidence on a vertical axis, from low to moderate to high, and experience on a horizontal axis, from limited to extensive. The working model demonstrates five levels of authority placed according to one's level of experience (1–9) and the confidence others have in his or her abilities (1–9). The levels of authority are represented as follows:

1. Rookie (1, 1)—limited experience, low confidence
2. Worker bee (5, 5)—moderate experience, moderate confidence
3. New member (9, 1)—extensive experience, low confidence
4. Rising star (1, 9)—limited experience, high confidence
5. Partner (9, 9)—extensive experience, high confidence (Figure 6.1)

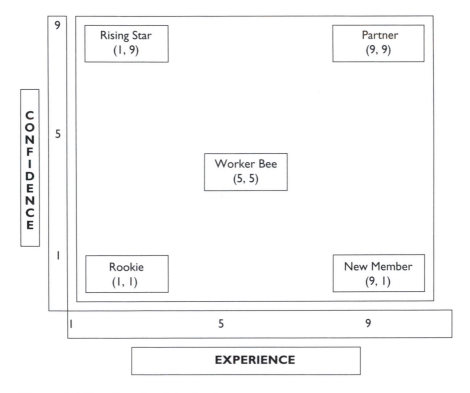

Figure 6.1 Five Levels of Authority

Source: Adapted with permission from Gilley, J. W., N. W. Boughton, and A. Maycunich. *The Performance Challenge: Developing Management Systems to Make Employees Your Greatest Asset.* Cambridge, MA: Perseus, 1999.

When delegating tasks and responsibilities, it is important to identify the appropriate level of authority. Employee experience and your confidence in his or her skills and abilities determine which level of authority is granted. For example:

- Rookie (1, 1)—At this level of authority, experience is limited and confidence is low. The employee gets the facts (e.g., gathers data, prepares data requests), but you as the coach decide what further actions are necessary. As the individual successfully completes assignments, your confidence rises.
- Worker bee (5, 5)—Experience and confidence are both moderate. The employee decides the actions to be taken, but you maintain veto power. This limits the employee's freedom until he or she has gained even more experience and the your confidence rises higher. Performance feedback and monitoring activities are still very important at this stage.
- New member (9, 1)—Although this employee's experience is extensive, you have little or no firsthand knowledge of the employee and thus have little confidence. Therefore, allow the employee to handle the task while closely monitoring performance. Feedback is not as critical here because the individual has performed successfully in the past. Monitoring future performance is the best way of increasing your confidence in the employee's skills and abilities.
- Rising star (1, 9)—At this level, experience is limited, but you have complete confidence in the potential abilities of the employee. In this circumstance, you work closely with the employee by training him or her, assigning tasks to be completed, and providing positive and constructive feedback about performance. Serving as a career advisor (one of the performance coaching and management process roles; see chapter 3) is most appropriate when working with this type of employee.
- Partner (9, 9)—At this point, experience is extensive and confidence is high. The employee is free to act and simply report results. Here the employee is operating on your behalf, at the highest level of authority.

Once the most appropriate level of authority has been identified, a few moments should be spent with the employee discussing possible performance barriers. Collaborative identification of ways by which performance barriers can be eliminated creates synergistic relationships between you and your employees. This conversation also gives your employees an opportunity to discuss more thoroughly the exact performance outputs expected.

Delegation as a Career-Development Strategy. An often overlooked performance-improvement strategy is that of delegating work assignments to employees to improve their skills and abilities. In essence, delegation implies that employees are valuable and trusted and capable of producing desired results, serving as replacements for other employees, and assuming others' tasks and responsibilities. Unfortunately, some managers fear delegating work to their employees. They contend that it takes twice as long to explain how to do a job task as it would to do it themselves. Others believe that employees will "screw it up." These weak excuses prevent employees from facing and mastering challenges that could lead to their growth and development. Performance coaches recognize the value of delegation in securing results through people.

Delegation is seldom recognized as a performance-improvement or career-development strategy. Yet by its very nature, it allows more-experienced individuals to delegate tasks and responsibilities to less-experienced employees, which gives them the opportunity to acquire new knowledge, skills, and competencies. Over time, the delegation cycle enhances the employee's performance capacity to such a point that he or she is able to take on even more difficult tasks and responsibilities. As the cycle continues, employees grow and develop, which enables them to become more important assets within the organization. Consequently, delegation is quintessentially a performance-improvement and career-development strategy.

Implementing and Managing Learning

Before providing training, identify the employee's knowledge and skills and determine whether he or she is willing to embrace the change. If so, the learning engagement has reached the commitment threshold. The commitment phase consists of three sub-phases: installation, adoption, and internalization.

During the installation period, the learning engagement is tested for the first time, sometimes referred to as the pilot-testing phase. During this phase, problems and difficulties surface, providing opportunities to modify and adjust the learning engagement. As problems and difficulties are resolved, a more realistic level of conviction toward the transformation develops, which allows commitment to advance to the adoption level.

During installation, some pessimism is common. Thus, performance coaches create a work environment that encourages dialogue, fosters open discussion, and allows for the expression of doubts and concerns. Such efforts facilitate and encourage problem-solving activities that build commitment.

The first opportunity for true, committed action arises during installation. In order to be successful, the learning engagement requires consistency of purpose, an investment of resources, and the subordination of short-term objectives to long-range goals. Two outcomes are possible in the installation stage: change is either aborted or adopted.

A considerable degree of commitment is required for employees to reach the adoption stage. During this subphase, learning is still being evaluated and elimination is still possible. Therefore, performance coaches require all employees who are working on the learning engagement to regularly update them on their progress. These updates should be done both formally (meetings or presentations) and informally (personal or small-group discussions).

Learning engagements are aborted at this stage for a number of reasons, including the following:

- Work assignment and duties change.
- The need that sparked the initial commitment may no longer exist.
- The overall strategic goals of the organization may have shifted and now do not include the learning-engagement outcomes.
- The sponsoring performance coach may have left the organization or been reassigned to a new position.

At the conclusion of the adoption stage, terminate the learning engagement or internalize it. Internalization is the period in which all parties (i.e., performance coaches and employees) no longer view the performance change as temporary. Once internalization occurs, the organization alters to accommodate the change. In short, after internalizing new knowledge or skills, the organization accounts for the new performance by altering its motivation and feedback systems. Over time, the performance change becomes a part of the firm's culture and is adopted as an expectation. Internalization of the performance change occurs when its philosophies are reflected in employees' interests, goals, or values. In other words, employees become deep-seated advocates who take personal responsibility for the success of the performance change. Internalization is also stronger than any mandate because it generates enthusiasm, high-energy involvement, and persistence on the part of employees.

Identifying Strategies for Improving Learning Transfer. Before learning can be translated into value for the organization, it must be applied to the job. Unfortunately, most employees are on their own after a learning event, and hence, learning is not transferred to the job. Many employees revert back to their old habits as opposed to struggling with integration of new skills and knowledge. Others neglect to transfer learning because they fear change, lack confidence, or perceive no payoff for trying new skills or knowledge. Still others fail because they delayed application of new knowledge or skill. Failing to execute skills properly or apply knowledge correctly will lead to the lack of learning transfer.

A profound reason for employee failure to transfer learning to the job lies with the failure of managers. Learning transfer often fails because of managers' lack of support or involvement or their failure to provide reinforcement on the job. Managers often fail to assist in integrating change, skills, or knowledge on the job, causing confusion and frustration on both sides. Consequently, much of the change is lost.

Learning fails when managers neglect to be positive role models, to establish adequate performance standards, to create work environments conducive to learning, or to realize that developing employees is their responsibility, or when they fail to link learning activities to strategic business goals and objectives.

Organizations contribute to the lack of learning transfer by establishing policies, managerial practices, procedures, and work environments that are inappropriate or nonconducive to creating or enhancing learning transfer. Some mangers even believe that employees are easily replaced, hence reinforcing the notion that learning wastes time. To improve learning transfer, performance coaches need to adopt several strategies before, during, and after learning acquisition.

Strategies before Learning Acquisition

- Learning readiness—Many reasons exist as to why employees neglect to acquire and transfer knowledge and skills to the job, the most egregious of which is their failure to adequately prepare for the exchange of new information and ideas. Thus, employees must be ready, willing, and able to learn before they can hope to acquire knowledge and skills.
- Self-direction—To enhance the learning process, employees must become self-directed learners, which includes being able to differentiate between the skills required in teacher-directed learning and those required in self-directed learning; viewing themselves as independent, self-determining, and autonomous; possessing the ability to relate to peers collaboratively; and seeing themselves as resources for diagnosing needs.

Strategies during Learning Acquisition

- Communications and language—Learning will be incomplete unless the language used is plain, understood, and common to the learner. Language functions as the instrument of thought. Words are tools with which we shape employees' minds. Because ideas become inculcated in words, they take the form of language and stand ready to be studied and known, marshaled into the mechanism of intelligible thought.

- Instruction—The instruction process is most effective when presenting meaningful, practical information in a problem-centered approach. The more practical it is, the better. Information should be arranged so that each step leads easily and naturally to the next. One idea or concept should be presented at a time, allowing employees' ample opportunity to integrate it with their existing knowledge. Further, information should be presented in a manner permitting mastery.
- Enlightenment—Learning is not about memorization and repetition of the instructor's words and ideas. Contrary to common beliefs, learning is more about the work of the learner than the work of the instructor. Learning comes by progressions of interpretation, which may be easy and rapid. No real learning is wholly a repetition of the thoughts of another. Quite simply, learning is the process of internalizing in one's own mind the truth to be learned and applying it in some form or fashion. This is referred to as enlightenment.
- Practice—Practice can be differentiated from application in a simple way. Practice occurs during formal learning activities conducted in safe environments that allow, and even encourage, failure. Although practice should be as realistic as possible, failures should not endanger others, diminish self-esteem, or result in loss of productivity. Practice need not be a concluding action during the learning process, but can occur throughout learning activities as new tasks and steps are introduced. On the other hand, application is the execution of new skills or knowledge under *real life* conditions.
- Review—Learning can be enhanced by rethinking, reviewing, reproducing, or applying the material, information, or content that has been communicated. Use feedback and frequent summarization to enhance retention and recall. Failure to incorporate feedback and review into learning activities could result in incorrect application of material or failure to apply it altogether.

Strategies after Learning Acquisition

- Application—Learning transfer can be greatly enhanced by adhering to one simple principle—people learn by doing. Learning by doing is simply a process of making application of knowledge and skill on the job—it's that simple. Research has shown that the most effective learning results when application on the job immediately follows initial training.

- Reinforcement and feedback—Employees are more likely to repeat activities when positive reinforcement and feedback occur. Reinforcement and feedback provide rich incentives for learning transfer by enhancing employee self-esteem and encouraging positive performance patterns. One of the best reinforcement tools is performance review, which allows you the opportunity to measure employee application of new skills and knowledge on the job. Incorporating evaluation of learning into the performance review and appraisal process communicates to employees the value and importance of learning transfer. If new skills and knowledge are being evaluated, they must be worth obtaining.
- Reflection—Reflection proves one of the most powerful activities in which employees can engage to enhance transfer and integration of new knowledge, skills, or behaviors. It enables employees to learn from their mistakes, understand to their own thoughts and feelings, cope with barriers within the organization, and plot strategies for future use and application of skills and knowledge. Reflection enables employees to consider their next opportunities to apply new knowledge and skills. Moreover, reflection allows employees to consider different situations in which their learning may be applied, as well as what they might do differently under current circumstances.
- Expectation, application, and inspection—Developmentally oriented coaches often discuss their expectations with employees prior to engaging in learning activities. They provide ample opportunity for employees to integrate new learning on the job. Furthermore, they assess whether the subsequent changes yielded performance improvement necessary for noticeable results. The three-way technique known as expectation, application, and inspection allows managers to guarantee that what they receive is what they expect while concurrently communicating to employees their accountability for improved skills and knowledge.
- Recognition and reward—Establishing a connection between performance growth and development and organizational rewards is the single greatest factor in improving individual achievements. The activities that get rewarded get done. Learning transfer, therefore, must be rewarded to ensure its success. By contract, failing to reward growth and development, which leads to performance improvement, will prevent learning transfer from occurring.

Some employees require a great deal of support or encouragement when using new skills or applying new knowledge, whereas others must relearn skills in a safe environment. As a trainer, you engage in several actions before, during, and after learning acquisition to ensure learning transfer. These become strategies for improving performance and guaranteeing that the time, energy, effort, and cost of learning new skills or knowledge is a positive investment for an organization.

Improving Goal Setting and Decision Making

Effective performance coaching and management activities improve goal setting and decision making. Performance coaches provide sound, convincing recommendations, present them persuasively, convince employees of the steps required to bring about lasting performance improvement, and involve employees in the decision-making process.

Performance coaches can improve goal setting and decision making by developing employee readiness and commitment to performance improvement. The following questions serve as a guide:

- How willing are members of the organization to implement performance improvement?
- Is upper-level management willing to learn and utilize new methods and practices?
- What type of information do members of the organization readily accept or resist?
- What is the attitude of members toward performance improvement?
- What are executives' attitudes toward performance improvement?
- To what extent will individual members of the firm regard their contribution to overall organizational effectiveness as a legitimate and desirable objective?

Performance coaches' and employees' enthusiasm for a particular recommendation also gauge readiness for performance improvement. This provides an instantaneous measure of interest, resistance, cooperation, resentment, or reluctance, and performance coaches can use these measures to decide whether to encourage a specific recommendation.

Facilitating Collaborative Problem Solving

One of the most common reasons for adopting the performance coaching and management process is to facilitate collaboration problem solving. In fact, organizations expect managers to solve difficult performance, managerial, and organizational problems routinely. Though problems vary from department to department and from organization to organization, the coaching and management process helps make certain that the identified problem is indeed the one that needs to be solved. Therefore, the majority of a performance coach's efforts focus on helping employees define the correct problem and then approach the problem in such a way that creative, useful solutions emerge.

Collaborative problem solving includes ways of resolving conflicts and problems that satisfy performance coaches, their employees, and the organization. Many conflicts within organizations occur as a result of unresolved needs or those that are in conflict with one another. Therefore, performance coaches should use a collaborative problem-solving approach to address and satisfy employee needs.

Building on Strengths and Managing Weaknesses

There is an assumption that fixing employees' weaknesses will improve their performance and enhance organizational effectiveness. In fact, the majority of all training activities are based on this myth. Quite simply, this assumption is false. Fixing a person's weaknesses only makes performance normal or average, not outstanding. Building on personal strengths and managing weaknesses leads to excellence.

Most training activities focus on "fixing" weaknesses, so many managers have the misguided perception that their job is to identify and isolate their employees' faults. Traditional performance appraisals are used to amass evidence that supports this belief. Unfortunately, this is one of the biggest mistakes managers and leaders make. A more effective strategy is to design career-development plans that enable individuals to build on their strengths and areas of expertise while managing weaknesses.

Four characteristics reveal an individual's strengths:

- Passionate interest in a particular activity or subject
- High levels of personal satisfaction when performing a particular task or activity
- Rapid and continuous learning
- Achieving exceptional results when participating in a particular task or activity[1]

Performance coaches, therefore, isolate employees' strengths and position them for success accordingly. This enables the creation of career-development plans that shift the focus from *fixing* weaknesses to maximizing strengths and *managing* weaknesses.

The first step in managing weaknesses is identifying them. Weaknesses are easier to spot than strengths because they have been pointed out to individuals most of their lives. Former teachers, parents, previous managers, and even spouses have been telling employees the things they do not do well. Certain characteristics highlight an employee's weaknesses, including the following:

- Slow learning on the part of the employee
- Inability to remember simple steps and procedures of a task
- Defensiveness regarding performance
- Avoidance of particular tasks or activities

Once weaknesses have been identified, effective coaches develop strategies that help employees manage their weaknesses. Three strategies prove useful in managing weaknesses: delegating, partnering, and preventing.

- Delegating allows employees to work on tasks and activities for which they are best suited, rather than those at which they are unable to produce positive results.
- Partnering is not matching one person's strengths to another's weaknesses. Rather, it combines two individuals' strengths together to achieve a goal. Complementary strengths may overcome any weaknesses individuals possess.
- Preventing is the process of allowing employees to exercise their right of refusal to participate in certain tasks or activities. The primary difficulty in executing this strategy lies in performance coaches' inability to be flexible when assigning work tasks and activities.[2]

CONCLUSION

The performance coaching and management process provides a vehicle by which managers, or coaches, work collaboratively with employees to create an environment of continuous growth and development that ultimately leads to enhanced performance. Coaches internalize the process; it becomes an essential part of daily life.

SEVEN

Performance Coaching Success Inventory

The Performance Coaching Success Inventory (PCSI) included in this chapter contains two parts. The inventory for competencies identifies your skill in establishing collaborative employee relationships, growing and developing employees, enhancing employees' self-esteem, and rewarding performance. The inventory for roles reveals your strengths and weaknesses as a strategist, trainer, career advisor, and performance appraiser. Evaluating current performance-coaching competencies and abilities exposes your overall strengths and weaknesses. This information establishes a baseline for developing a learning acquisition and transfer plan for overcoming your weaknesses while building on strengths.

To complete the performance coaching inventory "self report," read each question carefully, determine your response, and circle the most appropriate number on the inventory scoring sheet provided. The point value for each answer is as follows:

Never	1 point
Infrequently	2 points
Sometimes	3 points
Frequently	4 points
Always	5 points

Use the following process for both the success inventory for competencies and the success inventory for roles. Complete both sections of the questionnaire. Next, transfer responses from each to the corresponding scoring sheets. Enter the point values (1–5 points) on the lines in the "Points" row, which are below each of the numbers in the row titled "Items." For example, if you responded "sometimes" to item number 1, then you would enter a "3" (point value) directly below the number 1 on the scoring sheet. Total all points recorded for each competency or role area and enter the cumulative score on the "Total" line at the end of each row. Refer to the scoring sheets for the "items" statement (identified with numbers) under each of the four competencies or roles. After calculating the total for each of the four competency or role areas, enter this overall score at the bottom of the page on the "Grand Total" line.

PERFORMANCE COACHING SUCCESS INVENTORY—COMPETENCIES

Read each statement carefully and identify the response most representative of your actual behavior as a manager. Circle the most appropriate number provided.

	Never	Infrequently	Sometimes	Frequently	Always
1. I create a communications climate that is nonthreatening, comfortable, and conducive to sharing information.	1	2	3	4	5
2. I encourage a free exchange of ideas, opinions, and feelings in order to help employees discuss their personal and professional problems.	1	2	3	4	5
3. I provide employees with opportunities to achieve or accomplish work that is meaningful to them.	1	2	3	4	5
4. I recognize employees for their overall and specific contributions to improved organizational performance.	1	2	3	4	5
5. I openly communicate with employees to help them improve their job performance.	1	2	3	4	5
6. I share with employees my extensive knowledge of the organization.	1	2	3	4	5
7. I share power and control with employees.	1	2	3	4	5
8. I provide rewards and recognition when employees produce long-term results rather than short-term gains.	1	2	3	4	5
9. I encourage interpersonal interaction among employees.	1	2	3	4	5
10. I am willing to be responsible for the growth and development of employees.	1	2	3	4	5
11. I appoint employees to chair committees, task forces, or projects in which they can have influence over results achieved.	1	2	3	4	5

	Never	Infrequently	Sometimes	Frequently	Always
12. I reward risk taking and decisive decision making.	1	2	3	4	5
13. I accept employees as unique individuals with differing personalities and interpersonal styles.	1	2	3	4	5
14. I provide employees with information about the mission, goals, and strategic direction of the organization.	1	2	3	4	5
15. I attempt to develop a close, personal affiliation with employees.	1	2	3	4	5
16. I celebrate the successes of employees, such as promotions, certification designations, and specialized training.	1	2	3	4	5
17. I attempt to get personally involved with employees.	1	2	3	4	5
18. I am willing to serve as a confidant when employees have personal or professional problems.	1	2	3	4	5
19. I encourage employees to act on their personal values and beliefs.	1	2	3	4	5
20. I reward performance that produces the overall results needed by the organization.	1	2	3	4	5
21. I attempt to develop trust with employees.	1	2	3	4	5
22. I encourage employees to take risks in order to advance their careers and succeed within the organization.	1	2	3	4	5
23. I encourage employees to participate in decision-making sessions and develop action plans designed to solve problems.	1	2	3	4	5
24. I reward teamwork and cooperation rather than individual contributions and efforts.	1	2	3	4	5
25. I openly and honestly express my opinions of my employees' performance.	1	2	3	4	5

	Never	Infrequently	Sometimes	Frequently	Always
26. I use developmental plans to encourage employees' growth and development.	1	2	3	4	5
27. I share leadership responsibilities with my employees.	1	2	3	4	5
28. I use financial and nonmonetary incentives to reward employees for their efforts and contribution.	1	2	3	4	5
29. I attempt to enhance the self-esteem of employees by delegating work assignments that are rewarding and satisfying.	1	2	3	4	5
30. I allow employees the opportunity to grow and develop, even if it means that other managers will be advising or influencing their career decisions.	1	2	3	4	5
31. I demonstrate a willingness to accept individual differences among employees.	1	2	3	4	5
32. I reward employees when they meet or exceed my expectations.	1	2	3	4	5
33. I attempt to enhance employees' self-esteem, even when their performance doesn't warrant it.	1	2	3	4	5
34. I provide timely feedback of observed performance to my employees.	1	2	3	4	5
35. I encourage employees to obtain personal mastery of a competency or skill area (e.g., selling, designing).	1	2	3	4	5
36. I make certain that employees have the necessary resources to successfully complete a task or job.	1	2	3	4	5
37. I help employees improve their knowledge and skills in order to enhance their careers.	1	2	3	4	5

	Never	Infrequently	Sometimes	Frequently	Always
38. I teach employees how to adjust to the organization's political climate.	1	2	3	4	5
39. During periods of conflict, I encourage open, honest communication to maintain employees' self-esteem.	1	2	3	4	5
40. I make certain that employees understand how their work contributes to the organization's success.	1	2	3	4	5

Competency Scoring Sheet—Performance Coaching Competencies

Competency 1: Collaborative Employee Relationships

Item:	1	5	9	13	17	21	25	29	33	37	Total
Points:	—	—	—	—	—	—	—	—	—	—	—

Competency 2: Growing and Developing Employees

Item:	2	6	10	14	18	22	26	30	34	38	Total
Points:	—	—	—	—	—	—	—	—	—	—	—

Competency 3: Enhancing Employees' Self-Esteem

Item:	3	7	11	15	19	23	27	31	35	39	Total
Points:	—	—	—	—	—	—	—	—	—	—	—

Competency 4: Rewarding Performance

Item:	4	8	12	16	20	24	28	32	36	40	Total
Points:	—	—	—	—	—	—	—	—	—	—	—

Performance Coaching Competency Score—Competencies
(Grand Total) _____

40	100	120	140	160	180	200
(20%)	(50%)	(60%)	(70%)	(80%)	(90%)	(100%)

PERFORMANCE COACHING SUCCESS
INVENTORY—ROLES

Read each statement carefully and identify the response most representative of your actual behavior as a manager. Circle the most appropriate number provided.

	Never	Infrequently	Sometimes	Frequently	Always
1. I have ability to see the big picture and establish a vision for my employees.	1	2	3	4	5
2. When training employees, I consider carefully the information or material to be presented, and I identify its relevance to their work, interests, and experiences.	1	2	3	4	5
3. I provide recommendations to employees about their career-development needs.	1	2	3	4	5
4. I immediately point out employees' performance shortfalls, before they become serious.	1	2	3	4	5
5. I provide employees the autonomy and freedom to decide which problems to address.	1	2	3	4	5
6. I assign employees work that allows them to apply new skills and competencies on the job.	1	2	3	4	5
7. I help employees consider career options and alternatives.	1	2	3	4	5
8. I use performance standards or criteria to measure employees' performance.	1	2	3	4	5
9. I rely on my understanding of business fundamentals to achieve results.	1	2	3	4	5
10. When training employees, I present new information in a practical, meaningful manner.	1	2	3	4	5
11. I help employees make career decisions.	1	2	3	4	5
12. I clearly communicate the negative consequences of poor performance to employees.	1	2	3	4	5

	Never	Infrequently	Sometimes	Frequently	Always
13. I set priorities that are consistent with organizational and departmental goals.	1	2	3	4	5
14. When training employees, I present information in a step-by-step manner rather than all at once.	1	2	3	4	5
15. I pose hypothetical questions to employees to expand their point of view regarding their careers.	1	2	3	4	5
16. I confront poor performance in such a way (e.g., using conflict resolution and problem-solving techniques) that employees maintain their dignity and self-esteem.	1	2	3	4	5
17. I involve employees in the decision-making process used to improve individual and organizational performance.	1	2	3	4	5
18. When training employees, I present only one idea at a time and help them integrate it with their existing knowledge.	1	2	3	4	5
19. I help employees discover their underlying reasons for selecting their current career path.	1	2	3	4	5
20. I provide employees with a nonjudgmental description of the performance behavior to be changed.	1	2	3	4	5
21. I am a problem-solver who takes an active role in the decision-making and change-management processes.	1	2	3	4	5
22. When training employees, I use feedback and frequent summaries to facilitate retention, recall, and application.	1	2	3	4	5
23. I help employees examine the seriousness of their career commitment by posing alternative views for their consideration.	1	2	3	4	5
24. I disclose my feelings about poor performance with employees.	1	2	3	4	5

	Never	Infrequently	Sometimes	Frequently	Always
25. I have the ability to remain impartial regardless of my personal values and biases and in spite of an organization's culture, traditions, and vested interests.	1	2	3	4	5
26. When training employees, I provide a familiar frame of reference by presenting new information in terms and symbols they understand.	1	2	3	4	5
27. I share my own career decisions with employees to help them think about and carefully examine their own career options.	1	2	3	4	5
28. I clarify for employees the effects of poor performance on the organization.	1	2	3	4	5
29. I establish connections between other departments in the organization by communicating the value and importance of teamwork.	1	2	3	4	5
30. When training employees, I use a variety of instructional methods to arouse their attention and illustrate specific points.	1	2	3	4	5
31. I express confidence in my employees' abilities to achieve their career goals.	1	2	3	4	5
32. When a conflict occurs with employees, I listen carefully to what they are saying in order to understand their point of view.	1	2	3	4	5
33. I encourage collective, collaborative problem solving, in which team members strive to create win–win solutions to difficult organizational problems.	1	2	3	4	5
34. When training employees, I use terms, symbols, and language with which they are familiar.	1	2	3	4	5
35. I ask employees to identify their career goals and to explain their strategy for achieving them.	1	2	3	4	5

	Never	Infrequently	Sometimes	Frequently	Always
36. When a conflict occurs with an employee, I clarify what the employee is saying in order to understand his or her concerns.	1	2	3	4	5
37. I create working relationships based on trust.	1	2	3	4	5
38. When training employees, I present material so that each step of a task or skill leads easily and naturally to the next.	1	2	3	4	5
39. I help employees with their long-term career planning and development.	1	2	3	4	5
40. When a conflict occurs with an employee, I ask nonthreatening questions to better understand what he or she is trying to communicate.	1	2	3	4	5

Competency Scoring Sheet—Performance Coaching Roles

Role 1: Strategist

Item:	1	5	9	13	17	21	25	29	33	37	Total
Points:	—	—	—	—	—	—	—	—	—	—	—

Role 2: Trainer

Item:	2	6	10	14	18	22	26	30	34	38	Total
Points:	—	—	—	—	—	—	—	—	—	—	—

Role 3: Career Advisor

Item:	3	7	11	15	19	23	27	31	35	39	Total
Points:	—	—	—	—	—	—	—	—	—	—	—

Role 4: Performance Appraiser

Item:	4	8	12	16	20	24	28	32	36	40	Total
Points:	—	—	—	—	—	—	—	—	—	—	—

Performance Coaching Competency Score—Roles
(Grand Total) _____

40 (20%)	100 (50%)	120 (60%)	140 (70%)	160 (80%)	180 (90%)	200 (100%)

CREATING DEVELOPMENT PLANS

Development plans improve a manager's performance coaching competencies, build on strengths, or lessen weaknesses. The nine-step process for creating a development plan follows:

1. Compare your current competencies, strengths, and weaknesses with desired competencies (see the results of the performance coaching success inventories for competencies and roles). Competency areas that fall below minimum should become part of your development plan, as should plans to continually develop your strengths.
2. Identify learning objectives that serve four primary functions: (a) they define the desired outcomes of the plan, (b) they guide the selection of learning resources and strategies, (c) they channel the development and selection of learning activities, and (d) they provide criteria for evaluation of learning.
3. Identify learning resources and strategies, including both material and human resources. Examples of common resources include books, handouts, newspapers, journal articles, lists of suggested readings, employees, superiors, mentors, resource persons, peers, professional trainers, videotapes, and cassettes. The identified resources will be used in strategies, including listening to lectures, participating in discussion groups, going to the library or learning resource center, keeping a journal of your political interactions, reading book chapters or articles on the identified competency area, making observations, and reflecting on political interactions and engagement activities to decide alternatives, options, actions, and strategies. Several resources and strategies may be listed for each learning objective.
4. Develop learning activities that provide opportunities to acquire the knowledge, skills, and behavior desired.
5. Identify a target date by which each learning objective will be completed. Establishing a date provides you with planning parameters and forces you to use time more efficiently.
6. Implement the development plan. Sequence the learning resources that will be used during the development plan, participate in formal learning or training activities, workshops, or seminars, and take part in on-the-job learning activities.
7. Create an on-the-job application strategy in which you identify exactly where and how you are going to apply new knowledge or skills.
8. Develop indicators of improvement and accomplishment. Determine when you have successfully achieved your learning objectives.

Indicators can be expressed in terms of successful completion of tasks, observable behaviors, time measurement, and so on.

9. Provide rewards and recognition for the successful completion of your development plan. In this way, you receive an intrinsic reward for the successful acquisition of knowledge and skills. When learning is viewed as a developmental activity rather than a punitive action, this essential step motivates you to apply new skills and competencies on the job.[1]

CONCLUSION

Becoming a competent performance coach requires you to develop a strategy for continuous improvement, which can best be achieved by creating a development plan designed to enhance your competencies, build on your strengths, and minimize your weaknesses. Identify your strengths and weaknesses by completing the four assessment instruments provided, and then create a development plan using the nine-step process previously discussed. At the conclusion of this activity, you will have created a long-term development strategy useful in becoming an effective performance coach.

EIGHT

Resources

The rise in popularity of coaching has produced a wealth of information on the topic. The profusion of information and support supplied by books, articles, and organizations and discussed in chat rooms is overwhelming, and it continues to grow.

The following list of resources, although certainly not all-inclusive, offers a broad overview of the information available. Because coaching draws from and sustains so many disciplines, the resources below tap into coaching, change, human resource development, and more. As this exciting field continually evolves, so too will its resources and applications.

BOOKS

Bergquist, W., K. Merritt, and S. Phillips. *Executive Coaching: An Appreciative Approach.* Sacramento, CA: Pacific Soundings Press, 1999.

Block, Peter. *Stewardship: Choosing Service Over Self-Interest.* San Francisco: Berrett- Koehler, 1993.

Chambers, D. *Coaching: Winning Strategies for Every Level of Play.* Buffalo, NY: Firefly, 1998.

Collins, Jim. *Good to Great. Why Some Companies Make the Leap. . . . and Others Don't.* New York: Harper Collins, 2001.

Cook, M. J. *Effective Coaching.* New York: McGraw-Hill, 1999.

Crane, T. G. *The Heart of Coaching: Using Transformational Coaching to Create a High-Performance Culture.* San Diego, CA: FTA Press, 1998.

Deeprose, D. *The Team Coach: Vital New skills for Supervisors and Managers in a Team Environment.* New York: AMACOM, 1995.

Fournies, F. F. *Coaching for Improved Work Performance.* New York: Liberty Hall, 1987.

Gilley, Ann. *The Manager as Change Leader.* Westport, CT: Praeger, 2005.

Gilley, Jerry W., and Nathaniel W. Boughton. *Stop Managing, Start Coaching!* Chicago: Irwin, 1996.

Hargrove, R. *Masterful Coaching.* San Francisco: Pfeiffer, 1995.

Hendricks, William, ed. *Coaching, Mentoring, and Managing.* Franklin Lakes, NJ: Career Press, 1996.

Hudson, Frederic M. *The Handbook of Coaching.* San Francisco: Jossey-Bass, 1999.

Johnson, H. E. *Mentoring for Exceptional Performance.* Glendale, CA: Griffin, 1997.

Kinlaw, D. C. *Coaching for Commitment: Managerial Strategies for Obtaining Superior Performance.* San Diego: Pfeiffer, 1989.

Lucas, R. W. *Coaching Skills: A Guide for Supervisors.* New York: McGraw-Hill, 1994.

Martens, R. *Successful Coaching.* Champaign, IL: Leisure, 1996.

Peterson, David B., and Mary Dee Hicks. *Leader as Coach: Strategies for Coaching and Developing Others.* Minneapolis: Personnel Decisions International, 1996.

Pfeffer, Jeffrey. *Competitive Advantage through People.* Boston: Harvard Business School Press, 1994.

Roe, R., ed. *Coaching: The ASTD Trainer's Guide Sourcebook Series.* New York: McGraw-Hill, 1996.

Rogers, Everett M. *Diffusion of Innovations,* 5th ed. New York: The Free Press, 2003.

Salisbury, F. *Developing Managers as Coaches. A Trainer's Guide.* New York: McGraw-Hill, 1994.

Shula, Don., and Ken Blanchard. *Everyone's a Coach: You Can Inspire Anyone to Be a Winner.* Grand Rapids, MI: Zondervan, 1995.

Stone, Florence M. *Coaching, Counseling, and Mentoring.* New York: AMACOM, 1999.

Tice, L. *Personal Coaching for Results: How to Mentor and Inspire Others to Amazing Growth.* Nashville, TN: Nelson, 1997.

Tichy, N. M., and M. A. Devanna. *The Transformational Leader.* New York: Wiley, 1997.

Ulrich, David. *Human Resource Champions.* Boston: Harvard Business School Press, 1998.

Whitmore, John. *Coaching for Performance,* 2nd ed. London: Nicholas Brealey, 1996.

ARTICLES

Allenbaugh, G. E. "Coaching: A Management Tool for More Effective Work Performance." *Performance Improvement Quarterly* 5, no. 2 (1992): 2–12.

Aurelio, S., and J. K. Kennedy, Jr. "Performance Coaching: A Key to Effectiveness." *Supervisory Management* 36 (1991): 1–2.

Bell, C. R. "Coaching for High Performance." *Advanced Management Journal* 52 (1987): 26–29.

Bernstein, B. J., and B. L. Kaye. "Teacher, Tutor, Colleague, Coach." *Personnel Journal* (November 1986).

Bielous, G. A. "Effective Coaching: Improving Marginal Performers." *Supervision* 55 (1994): 3–5.

Buckley, T. "Coaching Is Tough Medicine: Are You Your Company's Biggest Problem?" *The Costco Connection* (February–March 1998): 24–25.

Caudron, S. "Hire a Coach?" *Industry Week,* 21 October 1996.

Chiaramonte, P., and A. Higgins. "Coaching for Hire Performance." *Business Quarterly* 58 (1993): 1–7.

Doyle, M. "Selecting Managers for Transformational Change." *Human Resource Management Journal* 12, no. 1 (2002): pp. 3–17.

Evered, R. D., and J. C. Selman. "Coaching and the Art of Management." *Organizational Development Journal* 18 (1989): 16–32.

Himes, G. K. "Coaching: Turning a Group into a Team." *Supervision* 46 (1984): 14–16.

Keeys, G. "Effective Leaders Need to Be Good Coaches." *Personnel Management* 26 (1994): 52–54.

Keichel, W., III. "The Boss as Coach." *Fortune* 201 (1991).

Kelly, P. J. "Coach the Coach." *Training and Development Journal* 39, no. 11 (1985): 54–55.

Kilburg, Richard R., guest ed. Special Issue on "Executive Coaching." *Consulting Psychology Journal* 48, no. 2 (Spring 1996): 57–152.

Rancourt, K. L. "Real-Time Coaching Boosts Performance." *Training and Development Journal* 49 (1995): 53–56.

Shore, L. M., and A. J. Bloom. "Developing Employees through Coaching and Career Management." *Personnel* 63 (1986): 34–38.

Snyder, A. "Executive Coaching: The New Solution." *Management Review.* New York: American Management Association, 1995.

Stowell, S. J. "Coaching: A Commitment to Leadership." *Training and Development Journal* 42 (1988): 34–38.

Sturman, G. M. "The Supervisor as Career Coach." *Supervisory Management* (Nov. 1990): 100–101.

Woodlands Group. "Management Development Roles: Coach, Sponsor, and Mentor." *Personnel Journal* 59 (1980): 918–921.

JOURNALS

Academy of Management Journal
www.aomonline.org

Academy of Management Review
www.aomonline.org

Advanced Management
www.cob.tamucc.edu/sam/amj

Group and Organization Management
www.sagepub.com (click on "Journals")

Harvard Business Review
www.harvardbusinessonline.hbsp.harvard.edu

HR Magazine
www.shrm.org/hrmagazine

Human Resource Development Quarterly
www.hrdq.com

Human Resource Development Review
www.sagepub.com (click on "Journals," "Business and Management")

Human Resource Management Review
www.elsevier.com (click on "Journals")

International Journal of Coaching
www.ijco.info

Journal of Applied Behavioral Science
www.sagepub.com (click on "Journals," "Business and Management")

Journal of Change Management
www.tandf.co.uk/journals

Journal of Management Development
www.managementfirst.com (click on "Public Sector," "Journals")

Journal of Managerial Issues
www.pittstate.edu/econ/jmi.html

Journal of Managerial Psychology
www.managementfirst.com (click on "Public Sector," "Journals")

Journal of Organizational Behavior
www.wiley.com (click on "Business," "General Business," "Journals")

Journal of Organizational Behavior Management
www.haworthpressinc.com/web/JOBM

Journal of Organizational Change
www.emeraldinsight.com/info/journals/jocm/jocm.jsp

Leadership and Organizational Development Journal
www.managementfirst.com (click on "HR," "Journals")

Organizational Behavior and Human Decision Processes
www.elsevier.com (click on "Journals")

Performance Improvement Quarterly
www.ispi.org/publications/piq

Personnel Journal

Personnel Management

Personnel Psychology
www.blackwell-synergy.com (select title from drop-down list)

Personnel Review
www.emeraldinsight.com/info/journals/pr/pr.jsp

Supervision

ORGANIZATIONS

Academy of Human Resource Development
AHRD, College of Technology
Bowling Green State University
Bowling Green, OH 43403–0301
419-372-9155
www.ahrd.org

Academy of Management
235 Elm Rd.
PO Box 3020
Briarcliff Manor, NY 10510-9020
914-923-2607
www.aomonline.org

The American Coaching Association
PO Box 353
Lafayette Hill, PA 19444
610-825-4505
www.americoach.org

American Federation of Coaches
www.americanfedcoaches.org

American Management Association
1601 Broadway
New York, NY 10019
212-586-8100 or 800-262-9699
www.amanet.org

American Society for Training and Development
1640 King St.
PO Box 1443
Alexandria, VA 22313-2043
704-683-8100
www.astd.org

Coach to Coach Network
www.coach2coach.info

International Association of Career Coaches
PO Box 5778
Lake Havasu City, AZ 86404
866-226-2244
www.iaccweb.org

International Association of Coaches
www.certifiedcoach.org

International Coach Federation
2365 Harrodsburg Rd., Suite A325
Lexington, KY 40504
888-423-3131
www.coachfederation.org

International Society for Performance Improvement
1400 Spring St., Suite 260
Silver Spring, MD 20910
301-587-8570
www.ispi.org

Society for Human Resource Management
1800 Duke St.
Alexandria, VA 22314
800-283-SHRM
www.shrm.org

Worldwide Association of Business Coaches
8578 Echo Place West
Sidney, British Columbia, Canada V8L 5E2
www.wabcoaches.com

Notes

Chapter One

1. Hudson, Frederic M. *The Handbook of Coaching: A Comprehensive Resource Guide for Managers, Executives, Consultants, and Human Resource Professionals.* San Francisco: Jossey-Bass, 1999.

2. Gilley, Jerry W., and Nathaniel W. Boughton. *Stop Managing, Start Coaching!* New York: McGraw-Hill, 1996.

3. Gilley, Jerry W., and Nathaniel W. Boughton. *Stop Managing, Start Coaching!* New York: McGraw-Hill, 1996.

4. Peterson, David B., and Mary Dee Hicks. *Leader as Coach: Strategies for Coaching and Developing Others.* Minneapolis: Personnel Decisions International, 1996.

5. Hudson, Frederic M. *The Handbook of Coaching: A Comprehensive Resource Guide for Managers, Executives, Consultants, and Human Resource Professionals.* San Francisco: Jossey-Bass, 1999.

6. Ulrich, David, and D. Lake. *Organizational Capacity: Competing from the Inside Out.* New York: Wiley, 1990, 40.

Chapter Two

1. Peterson, David B., and Mary Dee Hicks. *Leader as Coach: Strategies for Coaching and Developing Others.* Minneapolis: Personnel Decisions International, 1996, 14–15.

2. Whitmore, John. *Coaching for Performance.* London: Nicholas Brealey, 1997, 27.

3. Whitmore, John. *Coaching for Performance.* London: Nicholas Brealey, 1997, 31.

4. Peterson, David B., and Mary Dee Hicks. *Leader as Coach: Strategies for Coaching and Developing Others.* Minneapolis: Personnel Decisions International, 1996.

5. Hudson, Frederic M. *The Handbook of Coaching.* San Francisco: Jossey-Bass, 1999, 16.

6. Hudson, Frederic M. *The Handbook of Coaching.* San Francisco: Jossey-Bass, 1999, 16.

7. Gilley, Ann. *The Manager as Change Leader.* Westport, CT: Praeger, 2005, 33–34.

8. Ulrich, David. *Human Resource Champions.* Boston: Harvard Business School Press, 1998.

9. Hudson, Frederic M. *The Handbook of Coaching.* San Francisco: Jossey-Bass, 1999, 16–17.

10. Burke, W. W. *Organizational Development: A Process of Learning and Changing.* Reading, MA: Addison-Wesley, 1992, 183.

11. Gilley, Jerry W., and Nathaniel W. Boughton. *Stop Managing, Start Coaching!* New York: McGraw-Hill, 1996, 43–45.

12. Hudson, Frederic M. *The Handbook of Coaching.* San Francisco: Jossey-Bass, 1999, 127–128.

13. Hudson, Frederic M. *The Handbook of Coaching.* San Francisco: Jossey-Bass, 1999, 129–130.

14. Gilley, Jerry W., and Nathaniel W. Boughton. *Stop Managing, Start Coaching!* New York: McGraw-Hill, 1996.

Chapter Three

1. Gilley, Jerry W., and Nathaniel W. Boughton. *Stop Managing, Start Coaching!* New York: McGraw-Hill, 1996, 43–45.

2. Brookfield, Steven. D. *Becoming a Critically Reflective Teacher.* San Francisco: Jossey-Bass, 1995.

3. Simonsen, Patricia. *Promoting a Developmental Culture in Your Organization: Using Career Development as a Change Agent.* Palo Alto: Davies-Black, 1997.

Chapter Four

1. Mehrabian, Albert. *Silent Messages.* Belmont, CA: Wadsworth, 1971, 44.
2. Rogers, Carl. *On Becoming a Person.* Boston: Houghton Mifflin, 1961.
3. Knowles, Malcolm S. *Self-Directed Learning.* New York: Association Press, 1975.
4. Burke, Warren W. *Organizational Development: A Process of Learning and Changing.* Reading, MA: Addison-Wesley, 1992.

Chapter Five

1. Gilley, Jerry W. *Improving HRD Practice.* Malabar, FL: Krieger, 1998, 91.
2. Buckingham, Marcus, and C. Coffman. *First, Break All the Rules: What the World's Greatest Managers Do Differently.* New York: Simon & Schuster, 1999.
3. Clifton, D. O., and P. Nelson. *Soar with Your Strengths.* New York: Delacorte, 1992.
4. Rothwell, William. *Beyond Training and Development: State-of-the-Art Strategies for Enhancing Human Performance.* New York: AMACOM, 1996, 26.
5. LeBoeuf, M. *Getting Results: The Secret to Motivating Yourself and Others.* New York: Berkeley Books, 1985, 9.
6. Gilley, Jerry W., Nathaniel W. Boughton, and Ann Maycunich. *The Performance Challenge.* Cambridge, MA: Perseus Books, 1999, 151–152.
7. Peterson, David B., and Mary Dee Hicks. *Leader as Coach: Strategies for Coaching and Developing Others.* Minneapolis: Personnel Decisions International, 1996.
8. Bradshaw, P. *Management of Self Esteem: How People Can Feel Good about Themselves and Better about Their Organizations.* Englewood Cliffs, NJ: Prentice-Hall, 1981.

Chapter Six

1. Buckingham, Marcus, and C. Coffman. *First, Break All the Rules: What the World's Greatest Managers Do Differently.* New York: Simon & Schuster, 1999.
2. Clifton, D. O., and P. Nelson. *Soar with Your Strengths.* New York: Delacorte, 1992.

Chapter Seven

1. Gilley, Jerry W. *Manager as Politician.* Westport, CT: Praeger, 2006.

Index

About the Authors

JERRY W. GILLEY is Professor and Chair of the Organizational Performance and Change and Human Resource Studies Programs at Colorado State University. Perviously on the faculty at Iowa State University, Western Michigan University, and the University of Nebraska-Lincoln, he also served as Principal and Director of Organization and Professional Development for Mercer Human Resource Consulting. Currently serving as President of the Academy of Human Resource Development, he is the author, co-author, or co-editor of numerous articles and over a dozen books, including *The Manager as Politician* (Praeger, 2005), *The Performance Challenge, Beyond the Learning Organization, Stop Managing, Start Coaching,* and the award-winning *Organizational Learning, Performance, and Change.*

ANN GILLEY is Associate Professor of Management at Ferris State University and Vice President of Trilogy Consulting Group, a performance consulting firm. Formerly on the faculty at Colorado State University, she is the author, co-author, or co-editor of several books, including *The Manager as Change Leader* (Praeger, 2005), *Critical Issues in HRD, The Performance Challenge, Beyond the Learning Organization,* and the award-winning *Organizational Learning, Performance, and Change.*